Of Moose and Me

Animal Tales from an Alaskan Childhood

Of Moose and Me

Animal Tales from an

Alaskan Childhood

K. Brenna Wardell

Corpus Callosum Press
Hastings, Nebraska

© 2019 Corpus Callosum Press

K. Brenna Wardell

Of Moose and Me: Animal Tales from an Alaskan Childhood

All rights reserved. No part of this publication may be reproduced, stored in a retrieval system, or transmitted in any form or by any means, electronic, mechanical, photocopying, recording, or otherwise, without the prior permission of the publisher or in accordance with the provisions of the Copyright, Designs and Patents Act of 1988 or under the terms of any license permitting limited copying issued by the Copyright Licensing Agency.

Published by: Corpus Callosum Press

Text Design by: Corpus Callosum Press

Cover Design by: Miranda Schmidt

A CIP record for this book is available from the Library of Congress Cataloging-in-Publication Data

ISBN-13: 978-0-9996869-4-2

Distributed by: Corpus Callosum Press

Hastings, Nebraska

To my family

Contents

Acknowledgments   ix
Introduction   1
Alaska   4
Of Moose   5
A Moose Named, Yes, Bullwinkle   8
Great Land   11
Danny versus the Moose, or Bad Dog, Danny   12
Arctic Sky   14
Danny versus the Alaska Railroad   15
Chapel of St. Nicholas   17
A Dog Named Tok   18
MacDuff the Fearless   21
Metamorphosis   27
Of Birds, Blood, and Finding My Voice   28
Owl Man   31
Ptarmigans Sled Too   32
Trickster   34
Night's Messenger   35
Chico versus All of Alaska   36
Some of My Best Friends Were Chickens   39
Catching   42
Saucepan Bach   43
The Raven Herself   46
Of Goats and Great Escapes   47
Milking   52
Dark Heart   55
A Difficult Birth   56
Turning   61
Evil Ponies   62

Pache's Folly   65
We Told the Seasons of the Year In Fruit   70
Out Again   71
This Is a Dutch Rabbit   74
A Questioning Child   76
The Christmas Kitten   77
Cat   81
Pigs Before Pearls: A Journey to the South Pacific   82
Saipan   86
There Be Monsters   87
Above Cook Inlet   90
Me versus the Silver Salmon   91
Birth River   94
On the Slime Line   95
Abundance   102
Danger or Dinner Bell?   103
The Story of Brave Bear Woman   105
Afterword   106
About the Author   109

Acknowledgments

For Mum and Dad, for their good humor and grace in living with the mischief of three unruly girls and for teaching us their love of animals.

For my sisters Jen and Rachel, for being the best co-conspirators ever.

For the animals, domestic and wild, with whom we grew up for teaching us lessons, simple and complex, about love and loss.

For the state of Alaska, home of vast snow-covered mountains, icy rivers, and bright flashes of fireweed and lupin, and for the wonderfully warm, quirky people with whom I grew up—I miss you every day.

Thanks also to Eric Tucker, publisher and friend, for all your help and encouragement in shaping this book.

Introduction

I grew up in Alaska, a childhood that seemed normal to me but that still amazes many of the people I meet. Perhaps this sense of wonder occurs because so many myths have developed around Alaska and the Far North, from Native folklore to the days of Russian Alaska, and from Jack London's Gold Rush tales of dogs and men to the current fantasies appearing in film, TV, and the Internet of Alaska as the home of hardy fishermen and pilots, homesteaders and miners, and truckers and hockey moms amidst, of course, breathtaking scenery.

Growing up, I took the state's bounty for granted: complaining about the clear, cold air and water, the abundance of fresh fish and moose to eat, and all the hiking through and camping in that astounding scenery. The first complaint was not unjustified: it was truly ice-to-the-bone cold at times. The second seems foolish, particularly as the adult me considers we children's frequent whines of "Not salmon again!" while I yearn for a fresh salmon fillet for dinner. As far as the camping and hiking, even at the time I had to grudgingly admit that it was pretty wonderful, although made less romantic by the swarms of mosquitos that followed us; the fear of being nibbled by bears, whose scat on the trails offered a very material promise of possible peril; and the limited tech of our hiking and camping gear, which led to some long and uncomfortably lumpy, drafty, and very wet days and nights and allowed a surprise entrance by occasional visitors, such as the arctic ground squirrels who raced around inside our tent when we camped in Denali National Park.

The Alaska of the 1960s, 70s, and 80s, the time during which my American father and British mother raised their family, was an Alaska largely undiscovered by the world, a place with very much its own identity, a rich group of diverse, eccentric people, and a multitude of animals. One of the most remarkable elements of my childhood was the chance to spend so much time with animals both wild and domestic against the backdrop of Alaska's environment, an environment increasingly endangered due to human activity, from oil and gas development and transportation to mining, and, of course, climate change. Even tourism, now the backbone of Alaska's economy, is a mixed blessing, from the cruise ships that bring money to the state while despoiling its pristine waters to the many visitors who flock to Alaska's beauties but sometimes frighten and kill wildlife, trample on native plants, and spread their litter round the state.

These stories, and the poems that accompany them, detail just a few of my family's and our friends' animal adventures in the places we lived: first the city of Anchorage in south-central Alaska; then Juneau, the state's capital, in south-east Alaska; and then back to south-central: this time to the city of Kenai, on the Kenai Peninsula, where I spent most of childhood. These tales are as true as my memory can supply, tempered somewhat by time, space, and my mother's desire that I not bend the rules of propriety (not sure I've managed that, sorry Mum!). The stories focus largely on my happy memories, while the poems explore other, sometimes darker, elements of life in Alaska and beyond while engaging with aspects of myth and history. If my work, particularly the stories, tends to focus on the sunnier elements of life, the honey with little vinegar, it's because as I get older I want to focus on those memories, not the other, more painful, ones that I carry with me: that's the work for another collection.

Alaska

My bones thin white birch trees,
snow covered, spread with the rosy blush
of sunset as the short day ends.

My flesh small flowers with few leaves,
vast roots digging deep into mountain slopes,
sheltering from tearing winds under solitary rocks.

My eyes the pools at the edges of the river
where the salmon gather for companionable rest,
and the driftwood nests of white and copper eagles
calling out to mates as they swoop down, fishing.

My dreams giant whales breaching, then diving deep
into cold gray depths—leaving only the cry
of gulls, the lapping of small waves.

Of Moose

Moose are some of the more improbable creatures you will ever see: tall, spindly-legged, Roman-nosed, seemingly ungainly and yet magnificently suited for deep snows, cold lakes, and the varied environs of Alaska. Moose are ubiquitous in Alaska, or at least they were, their species declining as more and more humans move in and the trees and shrubs on which they feed are destroyed by development and climate change, while hunting and vehicle deaths increase.

Moose are massive, their size most apparent when one suddenly finds a moose looming in front of one. For many years there was a big display featuring a colossal stuffed moose in the Anchorage International Airport, a moose under whose belly I imagined I could have easily passed if only I could have slipped through the thick wall of glass. A note about this display: Alaskans love to stuff everything and then display it—the more public the location the better. For many years I have characterized the Alaskan decorating aesthetic as "dead animal art," and in my childhood it seemed that everywhere we went, from banks and shops to airport waiting areas, was full of bodies—in part or full—of dead animals, from moose and bears to beavers and owls. This particular airport moose was a more-than-usually stupendous example of his species, but moose are typically impressive, particularly the bulls with their massive racks and giant shoulders. And moose are not only tall, they are heavy—no wonder then that when a moose decided to take a day-long nap in some long grass by our house the imprint of the moose's giant frame remained in that grass for more than a year.

When I was a child there were always moose around, often when you least expected them. For example, trying to get our car down the driveway we'd often find a moose dozing in the middle of the gravel, perfectly unconcerned about the humans and their ridiculous need to get somewhere quickly. In fact, I think I only passed math in high school due to the many times my mother could not pick me up on time due to the obstructions of moose or other animal mischief (particularly on the part of our chickens and goats).

With their mixture of grace and ungainliness, moose gave me some of my earliest memories of delight. For instance, one of my greatest springtime treats was seeing the moose calves with their plush brown fur, ranging from light fawn to deep chestnut, lingering close to the flanks of their mothers as they grazed on the first new shoots of the willow trees, their supple muzzles moving over the soft green, their dark lips reaching for the tender shoots.

Moose are normally very placid creatures, but their massive size means that they can easily inflict damage if they are startled or angered, so we learned from an early age to be very careful around them and respectful, especially during calving season. A few people have been injured, even killed, by moose who have kicked or trampled them, sometimes as a result of foolish action on the part of the humans involved.

I've only been really close to moose a few times, and these have all been human-reared animals accustomed to human sights and smells. Once, I had a chance to feed triplet moose calves and, years later, I gave a yearling moose—quite unaware of his strength and potential for trouble—

carrots from my hand. In his excitement he nearly bowled me over, pursuing me with his soft, eager nose in search of more veggies. The story of this yearling—Bullwinkle Moose—begins my tales.

A Moose Named, Yes, Bullwinkle

Moose are gloriously endearing, walking that fine line between cute and ugly with character to spare. All moose are attractive to some degree, but baby moose are downright adorable—all long, slender legs and melting brown eyes. Sadly, many baby moose are orphaned each year due not only to predation by other animals but because of hunters and auto and train collisions. If they are found in time, orphaned moose calves are usually raised by wildlife conservation and rehabilitation organizations. When I was growing up, however, we had few or no organizations of that kind, so sometimes local officials would, with a permit, raise them: hence the triplet moose calves cared for by Dad's friend Abe, a Fish and Game officer, and the single moose calf named, unsurprisingly, Bullwinkle, who was taken in by Mark, another of my dad's friends.

I met Bullwinkle on a visit to Mark's home many years ago. When we pulled up to the house I saw what I thought was a slim brown horse in his horse corral. As we got closer I saw this was no horse but Bullwinkle, calmly watching our arrival. Bullwinkle had, I noted, a pretty sweet deal. The corral was large and the horse barn, empty since Mark sold the horses a few years back, offered a snug shelter from the wind and snow; it also had music piped in—Bullwinkle particularly enjoyed country music.

Mark let Bullwinkle out of the corral so we could meet him, and I nervously took a step back. While Abe's triplet calves were very young and not at all imposing when I met them, no larger than a good-sized Great Dane, teenage Bullwinkle was already the size of a small horse. Mark gave me a carrot and Bullwinkle came towards me, his eyes fixed on the treat. I held it out, he stretched his neck towards me, and his velvety nose grazed my hand as his mouth opened to reveal large flat teeth. He chewed the carrot quickly, his strong teeth crunching it in seconds, and then, growing boy that he was, he came towards me for more.

Unfortunately, I didn't have any more veggies. Bullwinkle started nuzzling me, his brown muzzle moving over my face and chest, his tongue lapping at my skin. Bullwinkle then got even closer, practically knocking me down as he searched for hidden treats. Mark rescued me by distracting Bullwinkle with some quickly discovered carrots and cabbage, and I tried to put my disordered clothes in order and wipe my newly wet face: Bullwinkle certainly left an impression.

I didn't get to see Bullwinkle again, but I heard about him from my dad, who chatted with Mark about his progress. Bullwinkle stayed with Mark and his family until he was a tall young moose, just starting to sprout a prodigious rack (the antlers worn by male moose). Mark noticed that Bullwinkle began to become more and more of a wanderer, leaving for hours, even days, at a time to spend time in the woods behind the house, but always returning home for treats. Then, one day, Bullwinkle didn't come home again. Mark worried about him, particularly when hunting season came around, but he hoped for the best.

One day as Mark neared home, he saw a large moose lying in the middle of his driveway. It was a male, for as Mark drove his pickup truck closer he could see its magnificent, heavy rack. He drove towards the moose, who got to its feet but remained in the driveway. Mark drove still closer, and the moose stood still, regarding him. Was this Bullwinkle? Mark couldn't tell. Now that the moose was standing, Mark could see the thickness of its neck and shoulders and the gleam of the sun on its glossy brown hair. The moose remained in the middle of the driveway, staring at Mark, who got out of the truck and walked towards the moose, uncertain about what to do. The moose then began to move towards him. Mark wondered if he should try to make a break for the house or get back into the truck, but he didn't have time to move as the moose came even closer, its eyes fixed on him.

Mark barely breathed as he watched the moose—a moving mountain of muscle and flesh, the largest moose he had ever seen—move towards him. He braced himself. The moose charged up to him, stopped on a dime, and then kissed Mark right on the face. It was a wet kiss—involving not only muzzle, but also a little tongue. It was indeed Bullwinkle: he had come home for a little rendezvous and treat session before heading back to the forest and, no doubt, a very busy breeding season.

Great Land

An arctic fox boxed with a grizzly bear,
and a bald eagle, with long curved claws
and copper wings, fished wriggling salmon
from a wide, jade-colored river.

A sticky moose calf, five minutes old,
all legs, suckled greedily from its giant mother,
and plump ptarmigans, like children, slid
down the smooth side of a snowdrift.

Once I saw a wolf across a lake, who,
alone of these, looked back at me.

Danny versus the Moose, or Bad Dog, Danny

Our liver and white springer spaniel named Daniel the Spaniel, commonly known as Danny, was definitely a character. While he was incredibly eager and loyal, other aspects of his personality, such as his general lack of sense, were less than desirable. This is amply illustrated by the following story.

It was a chilly day even though it was springtime, and my dad was visiting a friend who lived near downtown Kenai. After the visit, he decided to take a short walk with Danny in the nearby woods. Danny raced out into the woods and disappeared—only the fading sounds of his barks announcing his presence. The barks rang out, fainter and fainter but evidently excited, as my dad walked on, enjoying the peace and relative quiet.

Suddenly, he heard a sound, a huffing muffing sound that sounded like the heavy breathing of something very, very large. All at once, Danny returned, bounding quickly through the thick snow, his barks of excitement turned to a breathy whimper. He was not alone: my dad, cursing spaniels and their simplicity, now found himself being pursued by a very large and very ticked-off moose. Dad raced for the nearest tree and climbed into it, grasping the trunk and branches with his gloved hands as he struggled for balance. He looked down to see a whimpering Danny trying to get into the tree too as the moose approached, harrumphing with exasperation and rage. Dad managed to haul Danny up into the fork of the tree, a silver birch, and tried to be one with it as the moose circled, considering the advantages of an attack.

Finally, the moose gave up and went away, and my father slowly and carefully climbed out of the birch. No sooner did he reach the base of the tree and release Danny, than the spaniel was off once again into the woods. Dad sighed, exasperated; not only was he cold, but he was quite sore from his inadvertent tree hugging. He had barely caught his breath and begun to walk in the direction of the road and home when he heard the rising sound of whimpers and the crashing sound of a large, hard body hurtling itself through the snow. His body aching and his hands frozen, Dad nevertheless climbed the birch with speed, for Danny had not only managed to find, but anger, the moose. Once again, Dad grabbed Danny and hauled him up to his place in the birch tree while the moose, enraged, circled, hoping to trample someone.

What felt like hours later, the moose finally decided it would rather graze than squash; it headed back into the woods. Dad climbed down quickly and managed to grab Danny by his collar before he could race after the moose and begin the whole wonderful cycle once more. While Dad has not shared the words he used towards Danny during and following this incident, I'm sure "Bad dog, Danny" was the least of them. Cold and hungry, Dad finally headed for home and Danny, his docked tail tucked as far between his legs as it could go, followed him, probably still hoping that he could once more take on the moose, *Canis* versus *Alces americanus*, having learned, of course, nothing at all.

Arctic Sky

At dawn, a golden spider climbs
a blue wall; as the day goes on
he slowly descends to sleep
inside the permafrost.

At night, an arctic fox in her winter coat
curls on her side on the black ice—
a crescent; as the days go by she relaxes,
her shining silver tail covering
her soft nose—a circle.

The eyes of wolverines light the tundra,
shining stars low on the horizon,
searching for shudders of movement,
scenting the warmth of small rabbits,
of slow or injured birds—
they are hungry.

Danny versus the Alaska Railroad

My middle sister and I had left for college when my parents brought home Danny, whose name came courtesy of my youngest sister. The small, wiggling puppy did his best to seduce them all, and by the time I visited at Christmas, months later, he was a full member of the family, much more at home than I felt after my long absence. Abundantly blessed with sweetness, energy, and empathy, Daniel was, as the earlier story indicates, somewhat lacking in brains and sense. One of my father's favorite games was to grab a flashlight and shine it on the ceiling and walls, darting it back and forth as Danny ran in pursuit, barking furiously. He never caught on to the imaginary nature of those birds of light. When my parents sold our house and stayed with friends outside Alaska (commonly referred to simply as Outside), Danny went too, curling up underneath my mother's feet for the long trip down the Alaska-Canadian Highway (the Alcan). When my parents returned to Alaska, Danny joyously returned to Alaskan pursuits such as racing after my father as he skied, tracking ptarmigans and seagulls, and a new hobby, courtesy of my parents' move from Kenai to Anchorage, Alaska's largest city: chasing the Alaska Railroad.

The southern leg of the Alaska Railroad runs from Anchorage through scenic Turnagain Arm and then branches off, with one arm going to the town of Seward, famous for the Mount Marathon trail race, and the other to the tiny port town of Whittier. As it moves back north towards Anchorage, it intersects with the Coastal Trail: the long network of trails that skirt the coast and extend into many Anchorage neighborhoods. Near downtown Anchorage the Coastal Trail and Railroad run parallel, separated by a long metal fence. Many residents of the area thrill to the sights and sounds of the Railroad, but Danny felt a special fervor; when he heard it rumble into view, clad in the state colors of blue and yellow, its long body flecked with golden stars, he couldn't help but chase it.

The railroad engineers quickly got used to seeing a barking spaniel, ears flapping madly, running in pursuit, and they'd egg him on, tooting their whistle at him as they got closer, and tooting again as he broke into a run, racing beside the fence and the thundering railroad. Even when Danny became blind due to illness and seemed to lose much of the pleasures of his old life, the sound of the Alaska Railroad would make him bark with excitement and spring back to life, ready to challenge it, canine versus train, *Canis* versus *comitatus*, once more.

Chapel of St. Nicholas

Breathless from beach running, children
dance in the deserted Russian chapel:
bare muddy feet bounce on the floorboards,
disturbing winter's dust, rattling slightly
the priests' bones, buried underneath.

The little chapel shivers, its wooden walls
gray from salt weathering, its onion dome
faded pale blue and the little golden cross
long gone. The wood of its boards remembers
the incantations: first shamans' songs, then
priests' litanies, and then the final extinguishing
of both, so that finally only the wind in the spruce
can call back the people and their prayers;
the priest who now lives in the nearby house
is growing old: he will have no successor.

The chapel's floor once bent with the weight
of the believers, now its only companions
are the village children and their dogs
who burst in, all together, jostling and laughing,
to play at fencing with slender fireweed stalks
while the dogs explore the chapel's corners.

Too soon they are bored, and with one shout
the children throw away their broken swords
and, with a whoop, run back to the beach,
leaving the Chapel of St. Nicholas quiet again.

A Dog Named Tok

I've told a few stories about Danny, the third of our dogs, but for me the word *dog* always provides an image of our first dog Tok: named after a small town in eastern Alaska. He was a malamute husky, part wolf, with a soft/coarse coat of white and gray, a thick ruff of hair around his neck, and a bushy tail ending in a snowy point. He was a large dog, beautiful and dignified: at least he tried to be. There are pictures of my sisters and me as small children riding Tok like a pony. In these pictures the expression on his face mingles disdain and dismay, clearly asking the question, "Why do I have to put up with this nonsense?"

Despite his obvious dislike of playing pony, and all the other things we children no doubt did to him, Tok was patient with us and always gentle. He was supposed to be my father's dog, but when Dad came home that first time Tok just cowered at my mother's feet, unwilling to go to him. While Tok was perfectly fine with my father, as with us children, it was clear whose dog he was from that first moment: he put up with us, but he loved my mother.

Malamutes are famous for their strength on dog teams, and we repeatedly tried to train Tok to pull a sled. We discovered that he wouldn't pull unless we pulled too; my mother said it was obvious he wasn't a lead dog—he wanted to follow. There's a picture of all of us acting as sled dogs and pulling our red plastic sled while Tok sits in the sled, pulled by these not-dogs, so very content. Tok's canniness in evading his pulling responsibilities raises an interesting question, subject to some debate within the family: was Tok really clever in seemingly being unable to pull or work in any way or was he simply lazy? The question remains, but we know he was certainly capable of deception, as the following story illustrates.

Tok was, in effect, my parents' first child, and he lived inside our small rented house in downtown Anchorage until I arrived. There wasn't room for all of us, so Tok was sent to a doghouse in the yard. My mother was concerned about this transition, especially when she looked out the window and saw Tok shivering. Even though she knew that as a husky he was perfectly adapted to cold and snow, she still felt bad. That was until the day that she looked out at Tok when he didn't realize she was doing so, and she saw that he was not shivering at all: in fact, he looked perfectly at home. Tok had been playacting—the first, and certainly not the last, of our animals to prove adept at performance.

We children were devoted to Tok, and we often worried about him because, despite his size, he wasn't really a fighter, unless pressed. One of those occasions occurred when I was small, my sisters even younger, and we'd moved from Anchorage to the city of Juneau in southeast Alaska. One of our favorite activities in our new home, along with beachcombing, was to go on neighborhood walks, often passing a house with a large, vicious-sounding German shepherd who was secured in its yard with a long chain. Tok was nonchalant about the dog despite its snarls, aware to the nearest millimeter of the length of its chain. However, one day as we passed the house the dog raced towards us and didn't stop. Free of its chain, it went straight for me, and Tok engaged. Our mother dragged us home as we protested that she needed to intervene, saying firmly, "Tok can take care of himself." Sometime later Tok came home: slightly battered and out of breath but much better off than the German shepherd, who was never off his chain again.

When Tok rode in our boxy red and white Toyota Landcruiser he stayed in the back, staring out the windows or sitting directly behind the black plastic bench seat where we children sat. A favorite car game was pushing each other into the trail of drool that ran down the seat, courtesy of Tok as he panted, pink tongue lolling to one side, with what looked suspiciously like a grin on his face.

Tok slept out in the garage in an old packing crate, and he'd always wake up early in the morning and accompany us to the bus stop to wait for the yellow school bus to slowly come into view. However, as the years went on he was slower and slower out of the crate—and then there was the groaning. Some mornings we'd call him and hear nothing but a groan; we'd wait and call again, and then, finally, accompanied by a series of groans and an almost audible creaking, Tok would slowly appear. He could still revert to high-energy status from time to time, but as the years went on he was definitely slowing down.

Tok sometimes palled around with one of the neighborhood dogs, disappearing for hours at a time but always returning. One day, the neighbor's dog came back but Tok didn't return, and he didn't come home the next day or the days afterwards. We never found any trace of him. Perhaps someone shot him or he was injured somewhere and couldn't get home. Or possibly, like his wolf ancestors, he went on a final journey, out into the woods, to die alone.

MacDuff the Fearless

When I was around ten, we smuggled MacDuff home. MacDuff (aka Duffy or Duff) was a Shetland sheepdog puppy with whom we fell in love for his freckled legs and paintbrush tail. Those were his most prepossessing qualities for, like collies, shelties are not born with their long, lush golden and white coats; instead, puppies have short hair in relatively dull colors. In Duffy's case, he was a rather muddy brown, with just a ring of off-white fur around his neck and on his stomach to offset this drabness.

We had to smuggle Duffy home because my father decided after we lost Tok that we were not going to have a new dog, at least not yet. We children, however, were dog mad, and no sooner did we hold the puppy, the last in the litter, as he squirmed in our laps, licking our hands, than we were relentless. Mum agreed that we could try him out, and so we took Duffy home.

We waited for Dad to come home from our position in the garage, Duffy at our feet. Finally, the car pulled up in the driveway. Dad parked, got out, and then opened the garage door so that he could pass through the garage to enter the house. Unbidden, Duffy went towards him, eyes shining, his tail wagging so hard that his entire body moved side to side so that he looked like a tiny canine comma or a furry crab. He went right up to Dad and sat at his feet, gazing up at him intensely with his almond-shaped brown eyes. Dad stopped, looked down at the puppy, and then that was it: he stayed.

The first night, however, Dad was insistent that Duffy be trained to sleep out in the garage, just as Tok had done.

However, the puppy whined and cried so much that after a few hours Dad relented: the puppy could stay in the basement. I don't know if Duffy even spent the rest of the night in the basement, but from that night on he not only stayed inside but he lived upstairs, often spending his nights sleeping under my bed.

While it was lovely to have him so close, the arrangement was not without its drawbacks. As I lay in bed at night, waiting for sleep, I could hear Duffy's presence underneath, crunching away at his bones. Beneath my bed there was a veritable bone graveyard, a grisly sight that I tried not to remember as I lay there listening to *crunch, crunch, crunch ... crunch, crunch, crunch*. My mother's classical records would be in play, perhaps the lovely lilting sounds of Ralph Vaughan Williams's "The Lark Ascending," but as I drifted off to sleep the music would be mixed with, often overcome by, the counterpoint of Duffy and his bones, their material reality easily overpowering the music's delicate uplift.

Like Dad, Duffy was an early bird, and he enjoyed nothing more than coming into the bedroom to find you awake, then rushing in to lick your hands or whatever parts were not swathed in covers. As an inveterate night owl who finds mornings difficult at best, when I heard Duffy coming, announced by the jingle of his collar tags, I'd try to play dead, hoping I could fool him. Duffy, however, was determined. I'd lie in bed, attempting to keep every limb as stiff and still as possible, and I could feel him sitting there, scanning my body for any little tremor, his gaze boring into me. The moment I broke concentration and moved he'd be on me: licking my hands and, if I wasn't careful, the next move would be to jump onto the bed and thoroughly lick the rest of me.

Duffy's quirks were many and varied. For instance, he loved to travel in our Toyota Land Cruiser but, unlike Tok, he wasn't in the far back, drooling over the back seat, nor was he sitting on the floor or on our laps as Daniel the Spaniel would later do. Instead, Duffy would perch on the top of the front bench seat, digging his claws into the black plastic. His favorite part of the seat was the spot near to the driver's head: close to the action. We were impressed by his agility in reaching this perch and his determination in staying there, often through sheer force of will and claw. However, there were times when Mum or Dad went quickly around a curve and Duffy came off the seat and landed suddenly in our laps. This usually occurred when we were in our Sunday best, and Duffy's claws punctured several pairs of expensive, much hated, pantyhose. I think he enjoyed the view from his perch: certainly, he was never carsick, unlike my youngest sister—whose occasional bouts on summer trips meant time spent on the side of the road counting the Winnebago motor homes waddling past and trying not to be eaten alive by mosquitos.

Another of Duffy's issues was his hatred of fireworks. Like many pets, the Fourth of July was his least favorite time of the year. He'd spend most of the evening underneath my bed, even though the fireworks were usually only small squibs or sparklers that my father had brought home: given the amount of daylight in July, the town belatedly celebrated the Fourth with an elaborate, noisy display in late November, when darkness was guaranteed. MacDuff also hated balloons, and one only had to say the word "ball-oon," elongating the syllables for maximum effect and running a finger along the taut side of a balloon, and Duffy would be under a bed.

MacDuff's most significant hatred, however, was reserved for men in cowboy hats, for some unknown reason, and large dogs, particularly German shepherds and huskies. Unlike his reactions to fireworks and balloons, which led to a quick and definite retreat, this last hatred made Duffy become as enraged and aggressive as anything that stands less than two feet tall and weighs around fifteen pounds can be.

Duffy's hatred of large dogs stemmed from an incident when he was a puppy. We were away on a long trip Outside and we'd left him at the animal shelter in Homer, the scenic city south of our home in Kenai, as the shelter was managed by a family friend. Duffy had been there for several weeks when our friend's dog, a German shepherd, decided to act on his dislike of the newcomer. He attacked Duffy, tearing into his side. Duffy escaped from the dog and disappeared. Finding him gone, our friend had the police put out an APB, hoping for some help. There was no response for a full day, until a woman called the police saying she'd found a puppy sheltering in a pipe in the bottom of her garden. Duffy then had a police escort to the local vet's office.

The vet, a gifted surgeon, was relatively new to Homer. He didn't think Duffy would survive, for his skin had been peeled back like a skinned rabbit's and he was very weak. However, the vet cleaned him and sewed him up, attaching his skin with buttons. Our friend felt horrible about the attack and paid for the entire bill, which must have been substantial, and then he nursed Duffy until we returned.

When we arrived back in Alaska and picked up Duffy from our friend's place we were shocked to hear the story and see his long, twisted scar. His skin was always very fragile where it had been damaged, but soon the scar disappeared as his puppy fur was replaced by a glorious shaggy coat of red-gold and creamy white. He was so beautiful that strangers would often approach us to ask about him and to pet his radiant coat. Duffy relished the attention: he was, it must be admitted, just a bit of a diva.

Following the accident, we were relieved to find that Duffy's spirit remained the same—he was sweet and loving, although sometimes rather timid. However, he now harbored an immense animosity towards all big dogs, a hatred that left no room for thoughts of his own safety—or anyone else's. On several occasions we had him running alongside us while we were riding our horses when we encountered big dogs: that was when the trouble started. No sooner did Duffy see a husky or a German shepherd or any creature of that ilk, than he immediately went on the offensive. We had to boost him up to sit on the top of a horse to save him from his own berserker nature. From the safety of fourteen-plus hands high, Duffy would bark his defiance as we tried to prevent the horses from bolting or from kicking the dogs that milled around us, focused on the tiny gold and white menace.

Duffy's penultimate moment of big dog hate came when we were on the Russian Lakes trail, one of our favorite trails amongst the many great outdoor spots between Kenai and Anchorage. The ground was still snow-covered, even though spring was close, and so we had swapped our tennis shoes for cross-country skis. As we skied back from one of the lakes we came to a place where the trail divided, with a bridge in front of us. Duffy, as usual, was up ahead, and he crossed the bridge just as we sighted a sled dog team coming towards us. My father succinctly describes Duffy as having the heart of a lion but the brain of a peahen which, in combination with his big dog hate, may have led to what followed. For when Duffy saw the dog team he didn't run back across the bridge to us; instead, he ran down the ditch to the frozen stream underneath the bridge, easily crossing the ice. The sled dogs, seemingly incensed at the mere sight of Duffy, left the trail and ran down the ditch after him. Some of the dogs managed to cross the ice, but others fell in. The result was a melee of tangled dogs jumping, straining, and flailing on the ice. The howls and barks of the dogs were interspersed with the cursing of the musher because the sled had also begun to slide towards the stream, and it was now in danger of being stuck in the ice.

We started to move forward to help, but the volume and nature of the sounds from the area under the bridge led us to believe that our offers of help would only enrage all concerned. We beat a hasty retreat, but MacDuff lingered for a moment, surveying the remnants of the once-proud dog team with something that looked very much like satisfaction. Then he raced back to us and down the trail: heading for home.

Metamorphosis

I wish I were small again with breasts
that didn't need a bra, with feet
that didn't need sensible shoes,
without the weight of hips,
of stomach, of this life itself—

to be a ferret sliding under a fence,
or a caribou bounding over the tundra
with my slim beautiful legs raised high,
to be the lazy eagle at the bluff's edge
watching for small birds in the dusty brush,
or the bear wet with cold stream foam
fishing delicately with huge claws
for the zigzagging silver salmon flashes—

to be wholly animal, wholly alive,
a dirty, tired, contented little creature
burrowed in the warm hollow
of my mother's arms, listening to my father
spin out a tale as the molten gold spider
sun slides down night's web, fading gray,
and the owl children gossip and polish
their beaks, their claws, and speak
the stories only they can know.

Of Birds, Blood, and Finding My Voice

It was a bright, cold morning. I looked out the window of my parents' bedroom and I saw the snowy owl. I called to my parents and sisters, who came to join me. He was huge: a giant white shape on a bare branch of the old birch tree. It was the middle of winter, there was snow everywhere, and he blended in perfectly despite his size: at least two feet high. He sat facing us, but from this distance I could not see his golden eyes; I could, however, see the curve of his short beak: practical and deadly. He was waiting on that birch tree, so close to our chicken coop, for us to let out his breakfast.

The owl was beautiful in his snowy splendor and admirable, in a way, for his patience—who knows how long he had been waiting or how much longer he would wait—but I was not eager to provide him an easy snack. Besides, to provide him his meal would mean that I was letting down my guard of our chickens. Even though I was little, I was protective of our chickens: like our dog Tok, I felt they were our property and had to be safe-guarded. Plus, they were near-pets, many bearing names bestowed by my sisters or myself.

While Tok would usually protect our chickens from all comers, we soon learned that this protectiveness did not extend beyond our flock. One day, we were invited to dinner at the home of one of my father's colleagues, who also had a flock of chickens. We brought Tok with us, and after some time we let Tok out of the house, believing that he would behave well (and, after all, the chickens were inside a pen). However, when we finished dinner and left the house we found that Tok had managed to get into the pen and kill many of the chickens. We found him sitting contentedly in the pen's center, surrounded by white feathers and blood. My father paid for the dead chickens, and many months of apologies no doubt ensued. Needless to say, Tok was in the literal and figurative doghouse for a very long time.

Tok and I had to spend a good deal of time guarding our own flock because it seemed that everyone fancied a chicken meal. The neighborhood dogs, as well as any strays, would prowl round, looking for an open gate. Eagles would soar languidly over our house, eying the chickens below and calling to their mates, "Hey, look here." Hawks quickly darted in, hoping for a quick lunch.

Once, when I was quite small, a hawk took one of our chickens right in front of me. The chickens were outside their pen, scattered over the little hill near the chicken house. The hawk swooped down when I wasn't looking, and before I could even scream it had that chicken in its claws and was away. I don't even think the other chickens had time to squawk, though they sent up a hullabaloo afterwards and hid in the chicken coop or nearby bushes.

Another time, the chickens were loose near our house, and, as I rounded the corner of the house to check on them I saw that they were busily pecking about in the forbidden zones of my mother's flowerbeds and her vegetable garden. Suddenly, I saw a hawk dive down and try to attack a chicken who was scratching amidst my mother's prized sweet peas. I started screaming so loudly that the hawk, startled, flew away without a meal. The hawks never again tried to approach the chickens when they were near our house, and little me, only about seven years old, started to faintly understand the power of a voice—my voice.

The snowy owl waited for several hours on that branch of the old birch tree, barely blinking; finally, he ruffled his feathers, flapped his wings, and melted into the white sky.

Owl Man

Owl Man lives at the end of the road
His name is Mr. Dark-in-the-Trees

His beak is smooth obsidian
A soft short curve
His claws of yellowed ivory
Know the plan of the hunt

His eyes are two spinning wheels
Hypnotize with a turn of his head
Prick like thousands of needles
His feathers steel—thunder as he shakes
them—his voice a lightning bolt

If he sees you, he'll freeze you
So you snap like a spring icicle
So I stay away from the road's end
And I run home as quickly as I can

The echo of his voice
Frost-jabbing at my heels

Ptarmigans Sled Too

Alaskan winters are long, and the many months of seeing nothing but the white of the snow, the blue or gray of the sky, and the brown of leafless trees can wear on one. However, there's a great deal of beauty and wonder even in that limited palette, particularly in the glitter of fresh white snow under silvery moonlight or the blush of a sunset warming the cool sky and turning the snow shades of lemon and rose.

Beautiful as it was, the snow created a challenge to everyday life: blocking the roads, threatening roofs, and becoming a 24/7 temptation to my father, who loved a good snowball sneak attack. We did what we could around the house, such as trying to keep the driveway shoveled to some degree, but the rest of the yard was left to the snow, which could rise up to the windows or higher. One winter, the snow came up so high that when Daniel the Spaniel went around the house he could stop and look down through the kitchen window at my mother washing dishes. Sometimes the snow was hard enough for us children to walk on, but much of the time we disappeared into its depths, finding ourselves waist- or chest-deep. The blowing wind shaped the snow into drifts, covering some objects, skirting others, creating sharp curves and soft banks. And it was in looking out at the snow one day from the warmth of the house that I saw the ptarmigans and quickly called the rest of the family to look.

Ptarmigans are small, round birds with feathered feet who often travel in groups. In early summer we'd see them raising tiny puffball chicks, and in fall we'd notice them rising to the tree branches when we hiked to our favorite cranberry-picking sites. They are particularly precious to Alaskans because they are our state bird—they are also one of my favorite Alaskan sights. Like a number of arctic animals, including arctic hares and foxes, ptarmigans turn white in the winter, with just a fleck of black on their tail feathers. In the summer the females are dappled brown, black, and white, while the males add russet necks and white bellies to their speckles: their color changes allowing them to blend into the landscape.

I called my family to look that day because I saw something I'd never seen before: ptarmigans sledding. A small group of ptarmigans had found a gentle slope of snow and they were gliding down it, their downy feet blending with the snow itself. One or two birds lost their balance and took a tumble, but on the whole they were exceedingly agile. We strained our eyes to watch them—their small dark eyes and the black flashes of a few tail feathers vividly showing up against the white—until they moved off and we too moved: to sit in front of the fire in the living room, drink hot cider, and talk ptarmigans.

Trickster

The sledding ptarmigans of the previous story may have gained their mischievous, playful streak by watching another iconic Alaskan bird: the raven. I've long been fascinated with ravens, birds who are central to the landscape, literal and figurative, of Alaskan life. In Alaskan folklore, Raven functions as a Prometheus figure who brings fire to mankind. He also acts as a trickster: a creature who creates change in the world. In other legends, such as stories from Norse mythology, ravens are companions to the one-eyed god Odin, whose two ravens, named Huginn and Muninn, bring Odin news and sit on his shoulders. Certainly ravens are very clever, learning from watching their fellow creatures, including humans, and trouble-solving individually and as a group in order to accomplish their own secret goals. I'd often see them positioned in the top of the spruce trees, speaking to each other with their rough voices and regarding us with their glittering eyes, no doubt considering the many tricks they could play on us.

Night's Messenger

black feathers and black eyes
dark claws and dark voice

capturing the moon in my wings
the sun in my beak

tearing the flesh of the divers
the fruit of the river flowers

in the icy inner forest
I find the tracks of prey

on the gray sea's path
I follow my hunger

I sing to the world
hoarse and harsh
unloved, unwished

I am philosophical
raven on the edge
of the world

Chico versus All of Alaska

As I was going through some long-stored belongings a few months ago, I came upon a small feather, shorter than my little finger, with a quill barely thicker than a hair. The feather is a multitude of shades of green, from lime to near black, shot through towards its tip with a stripe of brilliant yellow. I recognized it immediately as one of Chico's tail feathers, a precious, fragile thing that I had saved long ago and, somehow, kept all these years.

Chico was my parakeet, named after the title character in the TV comedy *Chico and the Man,* a character played by the late actor Freddie Prinze. We brought Chico home from the pet store when I was around nine, and he quickly became a favorite for his lively personality: we loved to listen to him chirping and see him cock his head to one side, observing us with tiny obsidian eyes. Brilliant green and yellow, Chico was a splash of color in our living room, and a constant temptation to our calico cat Becky Lou who, no doubt, hoped that she could "disappear" him in the manner of my giant goldfish Alice, who was there in her fish bowl one day and then ... not.

While Chico primarily stayed in his cage, we would let him loose from time to time to fly about the living room and perch on the curtain rails after, of course, having carefully contained Becky the cat. One day, however, things went horribly wrong. Somehow Chico got out of his cage, and somehow Becky was right there, and somehow the door to the garage was open, as was the door from the garage to outside, and then Chico was gone. We searched all around the yard, calling his name. We couldn't find him anywhere, and it was growing dark. My mother tried to reassure me that he would be fine, but I knew that wasn't so. It wasn't yet winter, but it was already moving towards fall, and the nights were cool. And Alaska is a place full of dangers for a tiny bird: from owls and hawks to weasels and dogs, not to mention the weather itself. And Chico was not only tiny, but with his bright green and yellow coat he stood out like a sore thumb in the somber greens, browns, and grays of the yard and beyond: I didn't think we'd ever see him again.

The next morning, we went out to look for Chico and, amazingly, we found him, perched on a branch of a big spruce tree, his bright colors brilliant against the dark green. Somehow, despite the cold, the predators, the very real possibility of getting lost in the vast size of the Great Land—there he was. He was too high up for us to catch him, our ladders wouldn't reach, and the tree was impossible to climb, so we tried to lure him down. We brought out his food: he simply looked at it. We tried shaking some of his favorite toys at him: to no effect. Our stress levels rose, for we knew that every moment he spent outside was dangerous, and that we had to get him down somehow.

Finally, my mother began to speak. My mother is famous for her composure and her ability to speak with anyone about anything in any condition, from chatting with the Queen of England to soothing irate babies, and from quieting spooked horses to convincing skeptical cabbies that children should travel for free. Now, she spoke to Chico. She noted the weather and the predators and a host of other dangers. He listened. She spoke of a larger cage and fancy new toys. He cocked his head. My mother continued talking. Finally, she promised him that if he came down she'd make another trip to the pet store and, when she came back, she'd bring him a mate.

Chico looked down at us, his eyes glittering, and then, with a flutter of bright wings, he flew down to my mother and perched on her arm. A week later my mother was as good as her word: he had a new companion in his cage, a brilliant blue and white female. Chico had taken on all of Alaska and all of us: and he had won.

Some of My Best Friends Were Chickens

While many people consider chickens to be some of nature's least intellectually stimulating creatures, if they consider chickens at all besides as a menu option, I have long admired, even enjoyed, the company of chickens: in fact, some of my best friends were chickens.

My parents started keeping chickens not long after we moved to a house located some miles out of downtown Kenai. The henhouse was made out of two large wooden crates nailed together with a flat roof that had to be tarred from time to time to keep out water: one of my mother's least favorite jobs. The chickens had a pen of wire and wood; however, whenever we could we let them out to roam and take dust naps under the big spruce tree. As delightful as it was to watch them enjoy their freedom, there was always the problem of getting them back into their pen, which required an exquisite mixture of eternal patience and wily craft.

We had a number of flocks over the years, and while not all of the chickens stood out as individuals, many of them did. We quickly learned that it matters how many you have and how you raise them. We normally kept a small number of hens of various sizes and breeds as egg layers. However, my father once decided to buy some fryers, kept solely for their meat. All the same in appearance, a dull white, and raised only to be killed, these chickens never seemed to have any personality. They also seemed to be unhealthy from the start: spreading an illness that injured some of our layers, to our dismay.

After the less-than-positive experience of the fryers, we concentrated on keeping a richly diverse group of laying hens, with the occasional rooster added to the mix. For instance, there were the Aracunas with their blue-green eggs and fluffy cheek tufts (my favorite, whom I named Silver Streak, had muttonchop whiskers that could best an eminent Victorian). The tiny Bantams, who came in colors ranging from rich nutmeg brown to a glistening silver flecked with black, were another favorite. There were also exotic chicken breeds in glorious colors who bore wonderful names, such as the Buff Orpingtons, a lovely golden buff color all over; the Silver-Spangled Hamburgs, who were white with black polka dots and whom we children called, of course, the Hamburgers; and Speckled Sussex chickens: brown birds with white speckles who were as soft and round as the idealized hens of the perfect pastoral farmyard. Along with these more exotic breeds, we also had standard, reliable layers such as the Barred Rocks—docile black chickens with wavy white bars who are amongst the largest layers—and Rhode Island Reds, big chickens in a rich red-brown color.

Two of my favorite chickens as a young child were a Barred Rock and Rhode Island Red whom I named Bert and Ernie (all hail *Sesame Street*). One of the few times I remember my mother being really, really vexed at me involved these hens. I was supposed to be supervising the flock as they streamed from their pen to peck, cluck, and explore the great outdoors, finding chickweed and worms to eat; instead, I was busy reading and not paying any attention at all. Thanks to my inattention, the chickens soon began to drift around the side of the house, approaching my mother's beloved vegetable garden. I looked up suddenly from my book and found that the yard around the chicken pen was empty. I ran towards the garden, which was gradually coming to life after the long winter: the carrots raising their delicate lacy tops and the peas just beginning to emerge from the brown soil, their smooth light green shoots soft and moist. As I paused, taking in the garden, I saw the hens approach the peas. I should have moved to stop them or yelled at them; instead, I watched, mesmerized, as the birds moved down the line of peas, seemingly sucking them one by one into their beaks: one moment there was a little pea shoot gleaming in the sun and the next it was gone as if it had never existed.

When my mother found out that the hens had pillaged her garden, I was on the receiving end of an extremely long, hard stare, the kind that made me almost run in place with the desire to escape, and an extensive speech about being very, very disappointed. I deeply regretted the incident; however, Bert and Ernie were my special girls and I'm afraid I would have definitely let them go pea sampling again if I hadn't, from that incident onwards, been under the constant supervision of my mother, who was determined to see her garden finally come to harvest.

Catching

A childhood spent cornering chickens,
escaped from the safety of their pen,
against brush and the barn's corners,
letting them discover entrapment
before I grabbed their tails, pulled them
closer, folded their wings against me;
they always panicked until I put a hand
over their eyes, soothed them with darkness.

Once, as the chickens scratched in the dirt,
a hawk swooped over the nearby hill—
his arched wings glistened gold-brown,
his legs stretched, his claws reached out,
in one long glissade he lifted a fat hen,
glided upwards, was gone. I watched,
so caught by that dancer, his intent—
the slow waltz of pursuer and pursued.

Saucepan Bach

We usually had only one rooster at a time, and they were all personalities. The first rooster I remember was called Charlie, and he had the most beautiful golden neck feathers I've ever seen. Despite his long, curved spurs and giant frame he was very gentle, and we'd often stroke his soft back and admire his iridescent green tail feathers. When we lost Charlie we got a new rooster: Lindbergh, so named for his flying ability that was, for a chicken, prodigious (chickens not being known for being particularly aerodynamic). At the same time we had Lindbergh we also had a younger rooster, one of the chicks reared by Matilda, our prized broody hen. We'd named him Saucepan for his saucy disposition; since he was very petite, my mother added "Bach" as a second name: Welsh for "small." He was coal black in color and, seemingly from the time he emerged from peeping through Mathilda's soft feathers, exceedingly energetic. As he matured he looked more like a hen than a rooster, exhibiting little in the way of rooster plumage or behavior.

This changed, however, when we lost most of our chickens, Lindbergh included, in an evening dog attack. Amongst the few hens who survived by remaining safely in the chicken house, we found Saucepan. Seemingly just hours after the attack and the loss of Lindbergh he began to exhibit much more dominant behavior than we'd ever seen from him, and he began bossing the hens around (although the alpha hen always reminded him that he couldn't take this too far). Before long, he sprouted the beautiful neck and tail feathers of a rooster.

Despite Saucepan's new position he remained docile and friendly, and we frequently picked him up to stroke him. He also retained a peculiarity: he was always the first to go into the chicken house to roost at night. Whether his behavior was due to lessons learned from his narrow escape in the dog attack or simply a desire to be up at the peaky peak of dawn, we could never determine. Certainly, he showed great alacrity in darting into the chicken house at any sign of danger, never a mind to the hens' safety.

One of the best stories about our guests' experiences at our house derives from Saucepan Bach. One of my father's friends had had a bit too much fun downtown, perhaps trapped in the area that stretched between three of the town's bars, nicknamed the Bermuda Triangle (so called for how often people disappeared into it, reappearing with no memory at all of their adventures). He arrived at our house late at night, and since everyone was in bed he stumbled downstairs to the basement, where we always kept an extra bed for guests. He awoke at some point to strange, hoarse, alien cries, seemingly right by his head. Hung-over and confused in the dark basement, unable to ascertain whether it was day or night, he found the stairs and stumbled up them. He made his way to the kitchen where my mother, an early riser thanks to years with my dawn-loving father, was making breakfast. "What," demanded the guest, "is that thing in your basement?" My mother flipped a pancake and replied, "Oh, that's Saucepan our rooster: he has bumblefoot."

It turns out that Saucepan had frostbite on one of his feet and this had caused an infection; my mother, therefore, had brought him inside for some warmth and care, creating a temporary chicken house for him near the furnace, which resided in the unfinished part of the basement. The sound that so startled the guest was Saucepan greeting the morning—or at least the small amount of light that filtered through the slim basement windows.

In future visits to our basement the guest always made sure to check the surroundings for errant roosters before bedding down for the night. Given our tendency to put all manner of creatures in the basement for care, this was probably a smart move. The guest reportedly dined out on this story for years, regaling his friends with stories of Saucepan: the fearsome monster in the basement.

While Saucepan was a particular favorite, my sisters and I had many pet chickens, and we used to take them everywhere. We'd bring them into the house and let them sit on our laps as we watched TV, we'd take them with us when we went sledding in the nearby quarry, and my youngest sister once tried to take her favorite hen, a Speckled Sussex named Coffee Cake, downtown shopping. However, my mother discovered my sister's plan when she did a roll call of the car's passengers and Coffee Cake clucked loudly, announcing her presence underneath my sister's coat. So, Coffee Cake did not get to go downtown, but she still had free range over most of our yard and house. On a few occasions I caught my sister in front of the fridge, letting Coffee Cake choose a treat. She'd hold the hen close to the open fridge, moving her up and down and along the shelves until Coffee Cake clucked, showing interest, and then Coffee Cake could have a few bites of whatever she desired. Mum did not approve of this either, but with all three of us scattering in different directions to do who knows what she probably just gave up, hoping we'd eventually find new, less feathered, companions.

The Raven Herself

At night my wings stretch
out into the moonlight,
covering the starlight,
my feathers brush the pillows,
my bones stretch over sheets.

I perch above the castle,
sing with my rough voice,
I sit on a man's shoulder,
looking out into the world—

my black eyes, my black body,
my black beak tearing close
at the black flesh of night,
at the surface of the dark.

My neck is long and snaking,
my nails can clutch a ledge,
molting darkness on my pillow,
feathering my sheets, my nest—

I am a bird turning into an angel,
an angel who dreams into being
a body turning into a woman.

Of Goats and Great Escapes

My mother was only partially in luck: from playing with chickens we children moved on to playing with goats. Our first goat was a doe (a female goat) called Mischief, so named for her propensity for trouble. All goats have a yen for naughtiness, but some are real tricksters, and this was the case with Mischief, a tan Toggenburg goat we got as a young goat, properly called a kid.

One of Mischief's great moments of wickedness occurred when the goats, like the chickens, were loose in the yard, supposedly supervised by us children (note a pattern of irresponsibility on our part). Dad was cutting wood, bending down to pick up the logs from the pile, taking them to his chopping block, and then bending over again to split them in two, his face taut with concentration. Mischief observed the process and the sight of Dad bending down repeatedly, his backside facing her. As we watched we could see her thought process at work. Mischief gazed at Dad's backside, tempted, and then looked away. She looked again, so very tempted, but no, she shouldn't. Finally, there was very clearly a moment when she made up her mind. She broke into a run, reared slightly, and then butted Dad firmly on the backside. He went right over like a toy and lay there for a moment, dazed. When he rose, I was momentarily concerned for Mischief: he looked pretty upset and he still had an axe in hand. However, after he'd had a chance to take a few breaths he forgave Mischief, although I'm not sure he felt so charitably towards us: after all, we had observed the whole adventure and said nothing. Truthfully, the sight of Mischief first resisting and then giving in to wickedness was much too mesmerizing to interrupt.

Despite her playful nature, Mischief turned out to be an expert and devoted mother, so much so that when we would separate her kids from her so we could bottle-feed them (helpful to the human-goat bonding process) she would thrust as much as possible of her udder through the fence to feed them herself. In contrast, my goat Genevieve (Genny), a black and white French Alpine with a rather comically large pink nose, was decidedly uninterested in motherhood. She could barely be bothered to push her kids out, and when she did she clearly indicated that that was the end of her responsibility. She happily looked on as we bottle-fed her brood, firmly dismissing maternity with a shake of her head as she went back to eating: her favorite pursuit.

We had a sturdy two-story barn for the goats, made as part of a project with the local high school, whose students raised it in less than a day. We always enjoyed climbing up the ladder to the hay loft and dropping hay on unsuspecting people below or spying on the doings in the yard through the small window in the upper level: doings that included numerous goat escapes. While the goats had a sizable pen in which to roam, they constantly escaped the pen to explore, hoping to gain the garage where the feed was kept or the garden, home of my mother's succulent, ever-endangered plants. Genevieve was particularly adept at escape, master not simply of the immediate escape but of the long-considered master plan.

The immediate or quick escape usually consisted in a goat pushing past a human as that human entered the pen or fully knocking the human aside in the race to freedom. Genevieve, like the other goats, often indulged in this method of escape. However, she also spent much of her time plotting something better. The pen was made out of chicken wire that was held in place by a frame of wooden boards on the top and bottom; large wooden posts dug deep into the ground secured the frame, ensuring the pen's stability. Genevieve could not dig underneath the pen or leap over it; instead, in her most memorable escape she slowly, ever so slowly, worked to disassemble it.

It took us a while to understand her plan. I'd look through one of our home's windows and see her leaning against the wire of the pen, seemingly nonchalant, as if to convey, "Hey, I'm just hanging out." As I watched her over several days, I noticed that she'd lean much of her weight against the wire and then rub herself against it as if she had a particularly annoying scratch. When I visited the pen, I noticed that the wire had begun to bow out slightly away from the frame, weakened by the combination of Genevieve's weight and frequent rubbing. But I didn't really think much of this until one day the goats mysteriously escaped.

I happened to look out the bathroom window at the pen, only to find that there were no goats to be seen. We found Genevieve with her head buried in a sack of grain; the other goats were engaged in the annual springtime exercise of topping my mother's tulips. We rounded them up and locked them securely in the pen. Not long after that, we looked out at the pen: no goats, they had escaped again. We rounded up the goats and took a more careful look at the pen. It was then that the extent of Genevieve's plan became clear: she had gradually worked the wire free of the boards, creating spaces through which she and her fellow miscreants could squeeze. I had to admire the brilliance of the approach and the patience it required hour after hour, day after day, slowly working until that glorious moment when she could Steve McQueen it to freedom.*

When we weren't working to foil the goats' escape attempts, we were cleaning their barn, training them for goat showmanship, and grooming them. We were busiest in spring, because that's when the goat kids were born and we added bottle feeding and goat-human socialization time to the goat care schedule. It was extra work, but we didn't care because every spring we relearned a wonderful truth: there are few things more joyous than a goat kid at play. Because goats are prey animals, goat kids rise not long after they are born to feed, progressing to walking and even jumping with amazing speed. And, of course, they love to climb and butt. There was a small dirt hill near our house that was perfect for games of King of the Castle, and we'd all play, humans and goats, together. Attaining the top, I'd push the climbing kids on the tops of their heads as they pushed back, tiny hooves digging into the dirt. As quickly as I pushed them off the top they darted up again, ready to take the hill. Being butted by tiny kids is delightful, although a yearling packs a much bigger wallop as I discovered with Genevieve, who was too young to be bred her first summer and was able to remain an adolescent for a long time, playing with Mischief's kids and generally frisking about.

While dirt piles were a wonderful place to blow off steam, other heights were more problematic. Like many goats before and after them, our goats were fond of climbing on anything, including cars. They'd jump up on a car's hood and, if they could, leap onto the roof, surveying everything around them with great glee. The goats would

---

* See McQueen's character Captain Virgil Hilts, the so-called "Cooler King," from the 1963 film *The Great Escape*, directed by John Sturges.

then jump down to the ground from the roof or slide down the windshield to the hood, then launch themselves off it. A few little kids playing on a car was not a problem: they were too light to dent the metal despite their leaps, and their small, soft hooves wouldn't scratch anything. Genevieve the prolonged adolescent, however, was not such a harmless proposition that first summer we owned her, for she was as playful as a kid although as large as our mature females. I'd wince when I'd see her dancing about on one of our cars, fearing to find hoof-sized dents or scratches on the hood or roof. Trying to get her off a car was difficult, for she saw any intervention as another game. When she saw me coming she'd jump to another part of the car, often with a decided crunch, or she'd leap off the roof to the ground, using the roof as a trampoline for a mighty bounce followed by a magnificent flight towards the garage, the garden, or some other forbidden place.

One day, one of my father's police officer friends visited us, parking his cruiser outside the house. I looked out the kitchen window to see Genevieve on the cruiser's roof, nibbling its red and blue lights. As I ran out of the house, Genevieve slid down the windshield, her hooves, mucky from playing in the dirt, leaving long smears on the glass. I tried to grab her, but she danced to the middle of the hood and looked for a long moment at me, obviously enjoying the sight of me practically running in place as I tried to grab her. Then she bounded off the cruiser's hood with a great leap, punctuated by a whisk of her white/black tail, and raced down the driveway, easily far ahead of the silly human and her grasping hands.

Milking

Goats are a good deal of fun, but they are also work, especially during milking season, which lasts from the delivery of the kids in the late spring into the fall. During that time the does must be milked twice a day, every day. You can fudge a bit on the times but not too long, or the poor doe can get a painfully swollen udder or an infection such as mastitis. Here's a re-creation of just one milking session with my doe: the troublesome smartygoat Genevieve.

I lead Genevieve into the garage, my hand tight on her collar as she pulls, straining forward so forcefully she almost drags me head over heels. I use all of my weight to hold her back; the few times she has managed to pull me over has led to me looking like I was in a stampede. When we get inside the garage, I let Genevieve go. She runs across the concrete floor and climbs onto the wooden milking stand. She pushes her head through its wooden slats so that she can gobble up her grain in its red plastic bucket. I close the open slats, hooking them so that she can't escape. She doesn't even notice what I do—her mind and body are completely engaged in gorging herself on the sweet-smelling grain. I can see my breath and Genevieve's; it is cold this evening even though it is only late September.

I sit down on the milking stool, my body parallel to Genevieve's but facing the other way. I rinse a soft cloth in the bowl of warm water by my feet and then apply it to her black udder, washing away grit, sawdust, and straw. I extend my hands to her teats, wrapping my thumb and index finger around the top of each one. With these digits

I pinch the teats closed and then exert pressure with my fingers. Genevieve jumps at my touch—my bare hands are too cold. The milk flows from the teats in a jet of white. I squirt out a few jets from each teat to make sure the milk is clean and free of blood. I position the steel bucket and then begin to milk. Genevieve settles down as my hands warm on her udder. One of her teats is larger than the other because my left hand is not as strong as my right one and try as I may I can't seem to milk evenly. Because of this, I try to milk longer on this side, even though my left hand aches. The rhythm of the milk filling the pail soothes both of us, especially when the sound becomes muffled as the milk covers the bottom and slowly fills the pail. Genevieve chews quickly, turning her head to look at me with her gold and black eyes, then, scattering some of her mouthful of grain on the floor, she returns to feeding.

Overhead, the solitary bare bulb quivers, while the small radio emits its static song, which echoes round the unfinished walls of the garage with its assortment of gardening tools, car equipment, horse-riding tack, and grain barrels. The giant freezer against the wall, full of salmon and moose meat, emits a low dull hum. I almost fall asleep, leaning my head against Genevieve's warm side, feeling her internal beats of breath and digestion.

Soon, Genevieve's udder is almost empty: the plump teats have become dry and wrinkled. I must be gentle and not squeeze too hard or she will jump and upset the milk or get mastitis and have bloody milk. I hate to leave her with other people because they are not always so gentle, and they might not watch her reactions while they are milking to see if they are pulling too hard. Genevieve shifts her weight from one back foot to another and stamps a bit; she is getting impatient and wants to be released. She turns her head to look at me, and then looks hopefully at the full grain sacks in another corner of the garage. I get up from the stool and carry the full pail to the kitchen door, opening it carefully so the milk can't spill.

Inside, the kitchen's warmth is welcoming. I pour the milk through a syphon and filter it into two glass jars, then I snag a warm chocolate chip cookie from a batch cooling on the counter. The filter catches any hairs or dust that could have fallen into the milk, so that when I remove the syphon and filter only the clean bright white milk remains. I throw away the filter, put plastic wrap over the top of the jars, and place them on the top shelf of the fridge. All done.

Gloves and hat on again, I go outside. Genevieve jumps a little when I open the door, and her tail moves in anticipation as I walk over to the feed sacks and scoop up a bit of grain for a treat. She eats it from my hand, spilling half on the floor in her eagerness. "Greedy old thing," I whisper in one black ear as I wipe the remains of grain from my hand and unhook the slats. Free at last, Genevieve makes a dash for the grain, but I am accustomed to her tricks and catch her before she can munch anything. After a moment of girl-and-goat tag, and a little push-me, pull-me, I lead her outside and back to the barn. Once inside it, she goes straight to the manger, pulling out some wisps of hay as I shut the bottom of the Dutch doors and look in to make sure that our other doe Tessa, Genevieve's first daughter, is inside. Tessa is, and she's already asleep: curled up on the wooden table at the back of the barn. I close the top door and the barn and run back to the house for more cookies and, finally, sleep. But I'll be up at 7 a.m. tomorrow to feed Genevieve and Tessa and to milk again.

Dark Heart

ulu: a crescent-shaped knife traditionally used by women
flensing: slicing

The moon is a silver ulu
flensing the dark skin of sky:
full, thin, sharp, dull, opening
the flesh of the night.

The arctic lights are a curtain,
shivering red, green, and blue,
as a sleek bear shadow
silently glides towards seals
asleep on the drifting ice floes.

An arctic hare, done with day's
long journey of feeding and hiding,
hears ghostly music—caribou hooves
moving through snow—as hunters
wait in the soft curve of a drift.

A Difficult Birth

When I remember the goats giving birth, I recall the smell of the hay, sweet timothy, and the sawdust—its woody aroma mingling with the smell of blood. I remember too the thick membrane around each kid as he/she slid out into the world and the sight of the kids' small bodies—soft bellies, wet black noses, and tiny hooves shifting from jelly-soft to nearly hard in the minutes during which we toweled away the membrane and sopped up the blood. Then the kids would rise to their feet and head, unsteadily, for their mother, wisps of tail whisking in the air as they found the bulging udder and seized a teat. I also remember how soon those tiny hooves could outdistance me on the gravel road as the kids' minute, sinewy muscles and the beat of their new blood let them fairly fly over it ahead of lumbering me, and how easily they could, even taking time for aerial arabesques, beat me back to the barn.

Only one birth was not like this: the third of Genevieve's birthings. Her first was the twins Tessa and Tiger, a girl and a boy, and her second the triple threat of Arthur, Toddles, and Lambkins, all boys and future studs. All had gone well with these births: the sleek black and white kids delivered quickly onto the sawdust of the barn floor, the kids easily transitioning from anonymous membrane-encased shapes to distinct, quirky individuals.

On this day, this unusual day, Genevieve had played the pregnant mother to the full as usual: moaning with a volume and an intensity that only a goat of mine could do (she, like me, being much affected by the acting bug). However, something about this birth seemed different.

Genevieve had been so vast during her pregnancy that we were sure she must be having triplets. However, when Mum felt her sides she didn't feel the active kicking of triplet kids: only an occasional movement. Mum speculated that one or more of the kids might have been aborted and absorbed into its mother. In that case the remaining kid would be a big one—and very difficult to deliver. I began to worry about Genevieve and about the kid nestled somewhere inside her massive stomach. When Genevieve's backbone, near her tail, became soft, we knew the birth was near and my worry increased.

I was at school on the day that Genevieve went into labor. Mum checked on Genevieve, saw her condition, and realized, to her horror, that there was a problem: the kid was stuck. She alerted a man from the church across the road who had had some experience in animal births, and he came to help, but it was Mum who had to put her hand inside Genevieve and straighten out the baby. Finally, after her long labor, Genevieve delivered a single kid. Once born, the baby barely moved, and Genevieve, too tired to lick the kid or urge it to her udder, ignored it. Intent primarily on Genevieve's well-being, my mother didn't intervene; instead, she dried off the kid, bottle-fed it a bit of Genevieve's milk, and then took her, for the kid was a girl, into our house so that she could stay warm.

When I arrived home, I found Genevieve exhausted and listless in the barn and the new baby lying on an old towel on the kitchen's linoleum. Because of the trauma of her birth her large head was swollen, as were her long legs. Everything about her was, for a newly born goat kid, outsized, and I was amazed that only an hour and a half ago she had been inside Genevieve. I picked up the kid, cradling her in the towel, and she moved in my arms. I started to rub her swollen joints, pressing her against the warmth of my side. I took her into the living room and talked to her as we watched *Star Trek*, still massaging her limbs. Later, I took her outside and we sat on the lawn, its grass brown and dull as spring had only just begun. I propped her up on her ungainly legs, holding her for support. Then I balanced her on those long, swollen limbs so that she stood, momentarily, without support. Finally, I moved a small space away to test her. "C'mon, baby, c'mon," I said. She tried to come towards me, but she crumpled with the smallest movement. I went back to her, held her by the middle so that she couldn't fall, and moved her in a walking motion, trying to give her a sense of how to begin this process that had seemed so innate, so easy, to all our other kids. I then moved away again, trying to get her to walk just a little towards me. Finally, to my joy, she managed a few steps. She slept in my bed that night, a place none of our other goats had ever gone, and I held her close for warmth and massaged the long stretch of her legs.

  While we'd normally let the kids feed from their mother for a time after their birth, then began bottle feeding them to enhance their connection with humans, in this kid's case we began bottle-feeding immediately, making sure that those first bottles were filled with colostrum, the thick, rich milk that mothers produce for their young in their early days of life. To feed her, we started by dipping our fingers in the milk and then dripping the milk over the kid's mouth, catching her attention. Then we gently tried to insert the rubber teat, attached to its bottle full of fresh milk, into her mouth, carefully pinching the side of her mouth when she seemed reluctant to open it, making sure her mouth was around the teat and its dripping milk. It took the kid a little bit of time to realize that this teat was the conduit to that delicious milk, but when she did, and when I remembered to tip the bottle at the correct angle to ensure a steady flow, she fed with gusto.

Gradually, the little doe kid, whom I had named Gretel, learned to walk, her swollen head decreased to a normal size, and her vast legs became less awkward. Unlike all of Genny's other kids, who were black and white like their mother, Gretel was brown and white, and I loved to stroke her soft white belly and curve my fingers around her brown patches. As Gretel grew older, she revealed a personality that was even more rambunctious than that of our other kids, and because of her early stay in the house she seemed twice as friendly towards people and much less nervous of human habitations.

Due to Gretel's ease with people, she was one of the goats I brought to the mall one day to exhibit as part of a special animal presentation day. We set up a high pen around the goats, laid down some sawdust and hay, gave them grain to eat, and set up our information display. I was standing near the pen that contained the goats, answering some questions, when Gretel decided she was tired of being penned. One moment I was turning to answer a question; the next moment, Gretel was in my arms. She had somehow jumped the supposedly unjumpable pen and landed squarely in my arms, where she obviously felt right at home.

When it was time for Gretel to move on to a new home, we gave her to some family friends who treasured her devotion. This devotion extended beyond the regular parameters of goat-human interaction and it manifested in a number of ways, but particularly in our friends' morning runs. When the family went out for a run in the morning their dogs, anxious about being left behind, would follow, and so would Gretel: vigorously enjoying being part of a whole new herd.

Turning

The old gold leaves are heavy, damp,
the last cranberries almost hidden
beneath them—bright scarlet shapes
below a tracery of ice—the sunlight
cold, faint: the blaze of a far-off star.

I follow the path under the storm-
turned birch trees, find the soft brown
of the tender down from the inside
of an eagle's wing; in the quiet
I hear the echoing cry of geese
arrowing southwards—

    loneliness
becomes the quick shaft driving
the coming winter home—

    yet,
warmed beneath the moss, the seeds
settle, knowing that spring and summer
always follow the coldest
fall—

    a yellow leaf ends the moment,
touches my face as it drops to earth.

Evil Ponies

Ponies seem so cute with their bushy manes and tails, bright dark eyes, and rounded little tummies: all wrapped up in a diminutive package. Indeed, they are cute; however, they are also, as I have good reason to know, evil—or at least a number of them are (yes, I'm exaggerating a bit for effect here, but work with me). Think about this: have you ever been bitten by, stepped on, or otherwise maligned by a pony? Yes? Then you know that ponies may seem innocent, but they are really malevolent, if small, forces of terror in this world. When you think about ponies don't think, "Ah, adorable"; instead, your mind should scream, "Tiny capsules of chaos!"

When we were little, we children were always begging to ride Trigger, a Shetland pony owned by one of my mother's friends. Trigger had a glossy brown coat with underlying dapples, a creamy, shaggy mane, and a soft brown-gray muzzle. As his name indicates, while he seemed a rather innocuous creature he had a penchant for sudden displays of temper and unexpected trouble. For instance, I remember riding him across a field and having a perfectly nice time when, all of a sudden, for no reason at all, he began to shift his hindquarters side to side, to kick, kick, and kick again, and then to generally go in all directions at once. I was quickly off his back and down on my backside in the grass: grateful that I hadn't landed on something harder.

Trigger was clever: a dangerous characteristic of ponies, who, as a group, tend to be wily by nature. His owner had a barn that had a large door on one side and on the other side a Dutch door that was usually completely open for easy in and out access, but whose upper or lower section could be closed as needed. One day, my youngest sister was riding Trigger near the barn, having a very enjoyable time, and suddenly Trigger swerved inside the barn through its main door, galloped around its interior, and then headed straight for the Dutch door. The lower part was open but the top was not, and my sister abruptly found herself face-first in the door while Trigger, fully aware of the power of that Dutch door, burst through the lower portion to gambol riderless in the vegetable garden.

You would have thought that after our experiences with Trigger we children would have learned that ponies are trouble, but no sooner did some new neighbors arrive, bringing with them a new pony, than we were right there, breathlessly leaning over their freshly installed fence. We were excited at the new arrival's beauty: the pony was glossy black with white patches and she had a long, dark mane that she tossed with every step. Now, if we'd had any sense at all the pony's name should have told us everything, but just as we heard Trigger and thought not at all of sudden tempers or tricky stratagems, we heard the name Nightmare and didn't worry a bit.

We soon learned, however, that the new arrival's name didn't just refer to the color of her coat. Nightmare was a terror: you could barely go near her without getting bitten, but we still tried. My sister Jen did ride her a number of times, and, no surprise, Jen has proved in adulthood to be a master of extreme sports, as shown by her participation in cycle cross races, marathons, and triathlons: including two Ironmans. For the rest of us mere mortals, however, Nightmare embodied everything terrifying about ponies: maximum cuteness mixed with ultimate malice.

I have a theory regarding the evil of ponies: size. In an equine of a larger size, any potential for wickedness is distributed through long legs, a substantial expanse of rump and shoulders, and the lengthy stretch of an arched neck. But ponies are, by definition, small. They have minute rumps, minuscule shoulders, and small necks. From their tiny flinty hooves to their tossing miniature manes, they are the purest, most concentrated, form of evil. Luckily, the naughtiness of ponies has been contained in the past to their small spheres: a barn, a paddock, a backyard. Perhaps as a nod to their feisty natures, and the fact that they are, alas, often outgrown by any potential riders, a farm or corral seldom boasts more than one pony, although there are certain places, such as a fair, where a large number of ponies are collected to be ridden by visiting children. These ponies are always highly supervised—with good reason. Who knows what might happen if the ponies combined? What might these compact capsules of extreme cuteness visit upon an unsuspecting world?

Pache's Folly

I first saw the mare we'd call Pache on a chilly winter day. She was a dirty gold in color, her white face—a marking referred to as bald in the equine world—highlighting her two blue eyes. Because it was the midst of winter she had a shaggy winter coat, and her breath rose from her soft white muzzle. She was in a small corral behind a house that gave her space for only a limited trot around its circumference. She was small for a horse—only just over fourteen hands—and she seemed friendly, or at least not overtly aggressive, as I put my foot in the saddle and swung my leg over her back. We all tried riding her and we agreed: she was the one.

Soon, she came to live with us—mistress of a new wooden barn, topped with a rigid plastic roof, that still smelled deliciously of sawdust and of a large corral. She quickly became comfortable in her new home—particularly her barn, to which she quickly retreated at the first sign of rain. As the weather warmed she began to lose her shaggy coat, which was replaced by a darker gold/brown coat that was short and smooth. She was quite lean when she came to us, though it was difficult to see this underneath that thick winter coat. Over time she began to fill out, and we delighted in brushing her glossy sides, tracing the long line of her neck, the slight barrel-shape of her body, and the soft hillocks of her rump. Her tail was white and gray, with bits of black, and we tried to brush it to smoothness, although despite our work it never had the creamy fall of the tails of the palominos featured in the many horse books and calendars over which we children pored.

We loved to ride Pache: she had the most comfortable back of any horse I've ever known, and her movements, particularly her canter, were smooth and powerful. She proved herself an able jumper, easily bounding over the ropes on the beach that led down to the fishermen's nets, as well as other obstacles, such as the downed tree that lay over the path down to that same beach. As the summer went on Pache seemed to thrive, putting on more weight and displaying an agile mind (example: her escapes, described later). To aid such development my sisters and I grazed her at several fields some distance from our house, riding her down to the chosen field, walking back, and then returning several hours later to ride her back home. When we were lazy and decided to let her graze around our own house, we'd often balance on her back and pretend to be circus acrobats, surveying the garden around us. At other times we'd take it in turn to lie on her back as she cropped the grass, gazing up at the sky and the clouds scudding across it, marveling at this new perspective as we felt her muscles shifting under us. To work on her jumping skills we set up impromptu jumping obstacles, delighting at how quickly she took to this exercise, and we even took her to a horse show and displayed her in horse showmanship. Pache took all these new pursuits in stride, and she seemed as pleased as we did with her showmanship award: a blue rosette.

One day I went out in the morning, as usual, to feed Pache. I carried the large white bucket with her grain, and as I approached the corral I looked for her. Pache normally greeted me at the fence; if she was instead inside the barn, she'd quickly trot towards me and then move to her large rubber food container, waiting for me to climb through the fence and pour the sweet-smelling grain into it. That morning, however, I didn't see Pache in the corral as I approached it; instead, she appeared to be in the barn, although there was no rain or any other reason that I could see why she'd shelter there. I called and shook the grain bucket as I came closer, and Pache finally moved out of the barn and towards me. I stopped short of the corral's fence and Pache stopped too. I looked at her: something was strange. I counted legs: one, two, three, four, five, six … wait, that's wrong. I tried again: one, two, three, four, five, six, seven, eight. At that moment, a shape moved to Pache's side and I took in the owner of those extra feet: a tiny chestnut foal with patches of white.

I don't remember if I even had the presence of mind to fill Pache's food container before I went running up the gravel of the driveway, yelling out before I even entered the kitchen where my mother was making breakfast: "Pache has a foal, Pache has a foal!" My mother is a very calm and even-tempered person: a useful talent in a family where divaesque excitation is not unusual (I'm guilty of a good deal of such excitation). My mother regarded me quizzically for a moment, turning over a fried egg as I repeated my breathless, almost hysterical, refrain: "Pache has a foal, Pache has a foal!" "Wake your sister," she said. Jen wasn't home but Rachel was, and I feared waking her. Young Rachel was a deep sleeper who normally responded viciously to being awoken, as I knew well, having failed to avoid her right hook on a few occasions. This time, however, I prefaced the normal waking ritual with my cry, "Pache has a foal!" I had never seen Rachel arise so quickly: in a second she was up, and we all raced back to the corral. There was Pache, perfectly content, swishing her tail slightly as the foal nursed from her. Somehow, she'd managed to deliver the foal, clean it, urge it to its feet, and nurse it as we slept: nature perfectly at work.

In retrospect, Pache's seemingly spontaneous generation was not completely unexpected: there had been clues. While her owner assured my mother when we bought Pache that she had not been bred, she had been boarded some months back at a farm with a stallion, though of course they were in separate areas. When we later learned the extent of Pache's breakout skills, the idea that she had been able to escape her pen and find the stallion seemed less than impossible. Pache was a girl with definite needs, and she was not afraid to trumpet those needs, as I learned once when I rode her near a stallion at a fair. She was too much of a class act to actually rush the stallion, but there was a great deal of whinnying and some significant tail flair.

And there had been hints that her swelling belly was due to something besides a love of high-quality feed. Once, riding along the road to Pache's usual grazing area, a man yelled out congratulations from his car, puzzling me; in another instance, I was riding Pache at a fair and someone inquired when she was due. However, we believed the owner and her assurance that nothing could possibly have happened, and Pache had been quite skinny when she arrived and under exercised, so this was just meat and muscle she was putting on, right?

When it turned out otherwise, I felt particularly guilty, as I had ridden Pache at a canter just hours before that nighttime delivery—I'd even jumped her—and she seemed just the same, though possibly all that exercise brought on the delivery. We were very lucky that Pache had no trouble with the birth, as given our cluelessness, coupled with the time of her labor, there would have been no one to assist her. We named the foal Pache's Folly—Folly for short—and we were much more careful of Pache's virtue from then on, despite Pache's best efforts.

We Told the Seasons of the Year in Fruit

Small soft-skinned oranges from Japan
wrapped in tissue-thin green paper—
in December, every kid in school had them
in their lunch boxes; we'd stick the oranges
on our thumbs, like miniature pumpkins,
put the peel in the fireplace to scent the house.

In summer, there were plums—dark purple
with sweet yellow centers, green ones
with taut flesh—and wild strawberries, raspberries,
and blueberries; we'd come home covered
in scratches, dusty, tired, our telltale mouths
blue and red, our stained teeth full of seeds.

Fall brought apples, striped and fragrant,
taking up whole islands in the supermarket,
and the last of the rhubarb, tart strips in apple
pies, then nothing again until Christmas.

Now I can eat oranges in October, strawberries
in February, and fruits I'd only heard of—kiwis,
passion fruit, mangoes, and pomegranates.

But I still think of the seasons through fruit:
remember the miracle of those small orange
suns, each wrapped, a gift, when my world
was closed in snow, and ice, and darkness.

Out Again

One of the unfortunate side effects of Pache's intelligence was her tendency to escape. Perhaps the goats' constant Steve McQueening rubbed off on the horses, but Pache, like Genevieve, seemed to have a talent for deconstructing her corral. We'd wake in the middle of the night to the thundering of hooves as the horses circled the house, looking for snacks and having a good gallop. We all had the routine down: grab the torches and the grain buckets and move around the house shaking the grain in the buckets and calling out. Of course, by "we" I mean my mother, sisters, and myself: Dad absolved himself of all responsibility, with the result that we were the ones stumbling around in the dark in our nighties wishing that our horses would just stay put.

Capturing the horses was not an easy endeavor. Pache was too clever to come to the grain, but her white face and patches gave her away in the darkness—you just had to shine your torch in every direction until you caught that flash of white. Her partner in crime Tip, our second horse, was completely black, and she could have easily eluded pursuit simply by remaining in the darkness. However, Tip was both gullible and constantly hungry, so calling her and shaking the grain buckets usually worked beautifully.

The horses' escapes were normally nighttime occurrences, although sometimes they'd manage a daylight slip away and we'd get a phone call from a neighbor or hear a news story on the local radio of loose horses and, with a quick look at the empty corral, realize that once again Pache had found freedom.

Between the escapes of the chickens, goats, and horses, we were always busy. Years later, my father played on the familiarity of such escapes for his own purpose. He elbowed my mother in the middle of the night: "Elaine, the horses are out." My sleep-fogged mother rolled out of bed, put on her pink dressing gown and rubber boots, grabbed her torch, and made her way to the corral, only to find the horses were gone. She then circumnavigated the house, shining her torch in all directions, until, at some point, her brain came fully awake and she remembered: the horses were sold years ago. "April Fool's," my father crowed with delight as my mother groaned. Apparently, he managed to do this more than once. Despite such mischief, my mother never turned to any kind of revenge: a mark not only of her kindly, long-suffering nature and her British reverence for a joke well played, but a simple acknowledgment of the truth: she was always capturing critters—whether children or animals.

Despite his cleverness in fooling my mother, my father was not always aware of what was really going on at the house, while my mother knew exactly what everyone was up to—animals human and nonhuman. For instance, my father was unaware of just how destructive our critters could be, whether taking out emerging vegetables, as in the Bert and Ernie incident with the peas, or topping the tulips just as they started to bloom, a favorite activity of the goats. When we sold the goats my mother hoped she'd finally get to see the color of her prized tulips, but that year the horses subbed for the absent goats—neatly topping each tulip around the house. A few years later the horses were sold too, and my mother really thought she'd finally see her flowers; instead, a local moose wandered by expressly to trim each and every one of them. Then, one year, all was quiet. Spring arrived, and the flowers emerged, blooms of yellow, red, purple, and orange unfurling from tight stems. My father gazed at the flowers and exclaimed to my mother, "Elaine, the flowers you planted are so beautiful." My mother didn't have the heart to tell him that the flowers had been planted more than a decade ago: until this spring they had never had the chance to bloom.

This Is a Dutch Rabbit

I've never had too much trouble talking in public. I can certainly get nervous, but I don't suffer from the paralyzing dread that other people often experience. That always made things much easier for me than for my sister Jen who, as a child, hated public presentations of any kind. My mother always said it seemed very unfair that when we had to do presentations, such as our 4-H work, Jen would labor for weeks sweating over the text of her presentation and her delivery of it, going over it again and again, while I would write something up quickly and not even bother to practice it but just wing it on the day. I remember doing a bit more work than Mum recalls, but it is true that I would usually get a blue ribbon for relatively little effort while Jen, despite her work, would not. Frustrated, my mother even tried talking to some of the organizers about this. They agreed that it was a problem, but I kept getting first-place blue ribbons and Jen kept getting second-place reds or third-place whites.

While I could usually keep any anxiety I felt about public presentations at bay or translate that anxiety into a cheerful, if somewhat manic, delivery, Jen's anxiety manifested itself in other, often more overt, ways. For instance, one year she did a presentation on Dutch rabbits at the local community college as part of our 4-H work. Dutch rabbits are a smaller breed of rabbit who are often kept as pets. Their most prominent feature is a thick collar of white fur around their necks regardless of whether the rest of their body might be midnight black, dove gray, or soft fawn. We owned three Dutch rabbits: I had the male,

Thumper, and Jen and Rachel the females—Whiskey and the delightfully named Captain Generosity.

On that day Jen had brought Whiskey—small, black and white, and very gentle—to be her presentation model. Jen's name was called, and she went to the front of the classroom and carefully set up her illustrated poster on the stand, her hands trembling a little. My mother carried Whiskey to Jen and placed the rabbit on the table in front of her. Jen gently put her hand on Whiskey to hold her in place and began her presentation, the one she'd rehearsed so many times: "This is a Dutch rabbit…"

Jen doggedly worked her way through her speech, and her audience listened with rapt attention, or so it seemed: they were certainly very quiet. As she neared the end of her talk, she heard a titter of nervous laughter. She finished and looked out at the audience; they were staring at her, their eyes wide. She looked down and saw the reason for their laughter. As she talked she had, without realizing it, pressed down on Whiskey, the rabbit becoming more and more horizontal on the table until she was splayed out under Jen's hand, limbs stretched wide: about as flat as a rabbit could be.

Regardless of her hard work and the extreme cuteness and flexibility of her model, Jen received a red ribbon for her Dutch rabbit talk and I once more waltzed away with a blue. Mum, ever thoughtful, tried to redress this unfairness by taking Jen on a special trip downtown to get a congratulatory chocolate-dipped ice cream. And, despite her impromptu squashing, Whiskey was just fine: although she was probably grateful that Jen never chose to use her as a model again.

A Questioning Child

I thought the world held answers—
that I could learn the code of winter ravens'
caws, trace the scattered notes of swallows'
nests, dark freckles on the pale bluff,
and understand.

So I crept over the forest's thick moss—
following rabbits as they raced
to their burrows, stuffing wild berries
in my mouth like a summer bear.

When it rained, I sought shelter
under fallen trees and imagined slim weasels
slipping through thick bracken,
speckled shells between small sharp teeth.

I found no clarity, only random moments—
when a blue whale breached in the gray inlet
or a porcupine, quills flat to its sides,
scuttled through a darkening forest
and Canadian geese
cut arrows through crimson—

Then I caught something soft and unspeakable,
held it close, like an injured animal,
and felt the slow beating
of an alien heart.

The Christmas Kitten

We were admiring the Christmas decorations at the shopping center in downtown Kenai when the local vet's children came up to my mother carrying a cardboard box. Inside was a tiny calico kitten, a mite of white, orange, and black fluff within the darkness of the box. They'd found the box in the parking lot outside. We never discovered why someone would decide to leave any animal, particularly such a young one, without shelter in the middle of an Alaskan winter, but the kitten was indeed abandoned and alone.

At that point we had two other cats and my mother knew that my father had forbidden any new animals; however, we children pleaded to at least take the kitten home. Mum reluctantly agreed, and the kitten was soon nestled in a nest of blankets in another box. Because she was so young, too young really to have left her mother, Mum had to feed her with an eyedropper, slowly and carefully dropping the tiny points of liquid into the kitten's minute pink mouth.

My mother's ministrations were successful: the kitten, now called Becky Lou, grew and grew and soon became, when we lost our other cats, sole queen of our household. Her fluff grew into long silky hair that tended to go straight up one's nose, so it was difficult to pet her for any length of time, although she was exceedingly affectionate and always soliciting attention. Unlike our other cats, who had been roamers, Becky was a homebody, perhaps because of the trauma of being abandoned as a kitten; while I often saw her prowl the circumference of our yard, stepping daintily between the birch and willow trees and carefully investigating the pink flowers of the fireweed and the tall spires of blue-purple lupins for the scent of other animals, she never strayed beyond it.

Becky's favorite napping place was the bathroom we all shared—except my father, who was master of his own bathroom. Our small bathroom was always very warm thanks to a very efficient baseboard heater that ran along one wall. Becky could often be found with her back against the heater, her soft white belly with its patches of burnt orange and deep black turned up into the air, legs dangling softly, completely relaxed.

While Becky was never a large cat, she had a very decided sense of her own presence and power and woe betide the animal—human or nonhuman—who decided to oppose her. Given her propensity for sleeping on her back, her glorious soft spread of tummy open to the world, she was a constant temptation for my father, who liked to pretend a deep dislike for her (despite a secret admiration and a camaraderie given their shared love of napping), and he would often lower his foot towards her belly with a growl, as if to squash her into nothing. From the get-go Becky paid him absolutely no mind at all, not moving a muscle when he did this and seeming to understand that my father was all bluster; instead, it was we children who would cause a commotion in yelling at our father to "Leave Becky alone!"

Through the decades of Becky's time with us there was a constant dance between her and my father, and I'm pretty certain it was clear to all who had the upper paw. This was also apparent when she was introduced to MacDuff when we first brought him home. Seeing her, the Shetland sheepdog puppy bounded up, eager, tail wagging. Becky let him get close and then, with one slash of a dainty white paw to his soft pink-brown nose, showed him exactly where he stood. Duffy let out a yelp of pain and, from then on, gave Becky her space, as did Daniel in his own time.

As Becky became older, arthritis made her slower and less agile, and she took to napping more and more. I'd find her in the bathroom, a shock of white fur against the heater, or next to the fireplace, splayed on my mother's hand-knitted rug. I never seemed to see her actually move from place to place; instead, she'd just be there, and I wondered if there was some sort of particular kitty power—a displacement of space and time—that allowed her to transport herself, in full napping position, seemingly magically from place to place.

Despite Becky's increasing age, there was one time of year when she seemed to ignore the years, becoming as agile, curious, and quick as a kitten: Christmas time. As if in honor of her birthday season, Becky gained a kind of immortality at Christmas, emerging from her near-constant napping to race around the Christmas tree; bat her paw at the chugging Lionel train, my father's boyhood treasure, as it moved around the tree on its tracery of gray-brown tracks; and shred any packages or ornaments within paw's reach. Walking by the tree I'd see a quiver of the branches, indicating Becky at play beneath it, or a piece of tissue paper or a partially empty paper bag would suddenly take on life, shivering and scuttling over the carpet. My sense of wonder at that season, a time of song, snow, and roaring fires, was always enhanced by the sight of Becky, suddenly not sixteen but mere days old, chasing invisible Christmas mice in a maze of packages underneath a once spindly, but now fluffy and enchanted, spruce tree covered with the soft glow of multicolored lights and the colorful, eclectic cluster of years of ornaments and memories.

pink belly under soft dusting
of white fur, curved

claws of ivory flexing
with your moods,

ringed tail ginger,
white,
black:

Cat

Pigs Before Pearls: A Journey to the South Pacific

Despite posing for many years as a pessimist, my father is a true romantic. When we temporarily moved, for the purpose of work and play, from our home in Alaska to the South Pacific when I was ten, he was determined to visit the island of Majuro. Nineteenth-century writer Robert Louis Stevenson had described this tiny atoll in the Marshall Island chain as "The pearl of the Pacific": we had to go there.

But first, we went to some nearby islands. Our first destination was Guam, the largest and most southern of the Marianas Islands and the final transfer point on our flight from Anchorage via Hawaii to the island of Saipan, where we'd stay for several months. The Marianas were and are controlled by the United States, and so my father and mother had not thought to bring passports for us children or any kind of documentation. This proved a problem when the local officials decided that perhaps we did not belong to them. The officials insisted on seeing some documents, and they would not let us leave until my parents somehow resolved the issue.

I remember sitting for what seemed like several decades in a small, hot lobby on hard plastic chairs while my parents argued with a chain of indifferent officials. Finally, my mother asked in exasperation why any sane person would travel for days, for at this time it had been several days, with three grumpy, whiny, squirmy children unless that person was indeed one of those children's parents and therefore forced to do so. Upon consideration of this statement, perhaps delivered with a slight edge in Mum's normally calm and cheerful voice, the officials acquiesced to this argument, or perhaps they simply wanted to go on a lunch break. Regardless, we were finally able to move on to Saipan, an island with a vexed history as first a Spanish and then a German colony, and as the site of fierce battles between Japanese and U.S. forces during World War II. We quickly began to enjoy the area's many activities, such as snorkeling off Saipan's largely undeveloped beaches and traveling to the nearby island of Managaha in a tiny glass-bottomed boat, delighting in the coral reefs and the flashes of color—deep indigo, bright yellow, soft greens, vibrant orange and crimson—of schools of fish in that clear blue water.

After those months in Saipan we moved on to a week on the lush jungle island of Ponape (Pohnpei), part of the Caroline Islands, where we enjoyed a day trip to the mysterious ruins of the vast stone city of Nan Madol and the discovery of a host of toads of many sizes gathered underneath the magnificently large and busy bug zappers at our hotel. As we explored the island, we met a number of people wearing traditional dress: women who were bare-breasted and clad in grass skirts and men in loincloths. We felt very overdressed in our shorts and t-shirts.

After our time in Ponape, we set out for the Marshall Islands and the small atoll of Majuro. When we landed in Majuro we found ourselves on a narrow island, in some places no wider than a road, that was subject to hurricanes or any kind of storm. It also became quickly apparent that it was not as my father, taken with Stevenson's poetic praise, had imagined it. I'm sure it has changed a good deal in the decades since our visit, but at that time the pale gold beaches were covered with glass, the green-blue water was polluted from the sewage pipes that emptied right into the lagoon, and the population seemed to have little other option for employment than serving as taxi drivers (I'm sure this was not really the case, although the taxis were amazingly pervasive). But it was when we got to our hotel that my parents panicked.

It wasn't long after we checked into the hotel and started to explore that my parents started talking in a worried way, their heads inclined to each other, faces concerned. They were worried about the gardener, who had been maintaining the grounds, carefully working on some shrubs, since we arrived. He was not dressed in a shirt and shorts or in a loincloth; no, he was naked: not just from the waist up, but completely and utterly naked. Our parents were anxiously conversing because they were worried that we children had seen the gardener. Indeed, we had, but we were quite unconcerned by his nakedness: we were just interested in following the pigs.

To that point I had never been all that fond of pigs. A pig had eaten one of our favorite chickens while we were boarding our animals at a friend's house and I held a grudge (the same pig later ate a rabbit, and then it was eaten itself—apparently, it was delicious). I'd always found pigs to be smelly, dirty, and decidedly lacking in personality, but this was not the case with the pigs in Majuro. They were clean, neatly shaped, and quite small, each one bearing its own unique multicolored coat in shades of rust, black, and white. Unlike other pigs we had encountered, they were not slow and vast but quick moving and slim as they rooted around in the small garden by the hotel. My sisters and I followed their progress with delight. And while my parents worried that we'd somehow been damaged for life by seeing the gardener gardening in nothing at all, we were neither worried nor impressed: we were just enjoying the pigs.

Saipan

I never understood history until I saw the bones—
slender and pale, close to the concrete bunkers,
graceful tibias and femurs, the delicate arcs
of ribs—scattered shapes below the banyans.

Fecund ranks of breadfruits and coconuts counter
the invasion of rusting tanks, halting their advance
up the soft white sand from the sea's silent blue—

beneath its placid surface bombers, their cockpits
a home for schools of angelfish, an occasional eel;
swimming around unmoving wings I wonder,
and refuse such wonder, as thoughts bubble up
like breath, what happened to its crew
so long ago, recite within the sea's quiet space
"Those are pearls that were his eyes."

There Be Monsters

As a child I was obsessed with monsters—real or imagined—from the Komodo dragons in my mother's *Time Life* books to pictures of sea and land dinosaurs. I'd pore over images of spiny backs, bony humps, and curving horns: fascinated and frightened in equal measure. For years I had nightmares of a giant *Tyrannosaurus rex* materializing in my bedroom, its tiny beady eyes directed at my bed, its tail thrashing against my yellow wallpaper with its pictures of sleepy cartoon turtles.

Our parents did their best to assure us children that monsters—from the extinct dinosaurs to the imaginary werewolves, vampires, and ghouls—no longer existed. When we pointed to very real creatures such as the Komodo dragons, we were told that they were far, far away, certainly not in Alaska, although they admitted that, yes, we had to watch out for the local bears, which might be interested in the odd nibble. However, we were safe—or so they said.

In summer we'd often go down to Homer, the picturesque city about eighty-plus miles down the Kenai Peninsula from our home in Kenai. Homer is famous as the furthest west point for Alaska's road system, thus its nickname: "The End of the Road." A pretty harbor city, Homer overlooks the many wonders of Kachemak Bay, which are best seen from the long sand spit, less-than-imaginatively referred to as the Spit, which stretches into the Bay. Our favorite place to stay in Homer was a hotel located right at the end of the Spit called, in another less-than-creative gesture, Land's End.

In those days Land's End was a simple wooden building consisting of a hotel and a restaurant that hugged the end of the Spit, its boards long weathered to a soft gray. The hotel part was dormitory style, with each room containing a number of bunk beds and bathrooms down the hall labeled "Gulls" and "Buoys." It cost very little for us to stay there, so we often rented one of those dormitory rooms, even sneaking in our Shetland sheepdog MacDuff a few times. It's now quite a high-end place, not the sort of place you could wear your old fishing boots around as we once did, but at that time it was much more bare-bones, yet always comfortable and homey.

Exploring the Spit was a significant part of any Homer vacation, including inspecting all the boats in the harbor and doing a little fishing off the pier. We children took turns casting out and reeling in, rarely catching anything. However, this was not the case on one memorable occasion. In this instance Rachel, who was just beginning to learn to fish, cast out and hooked something. She crowed with joy, and Jen and I helped her reel in her catch. But what emerged was not the silvery flanks of a salmon but something mottled brown and white, with long spines, bulging eyes, and a massive head with an equally massive mouth filled, it seemed, with teeth.[**] We all looked at the creature in horror for a moment. Then Rachel, mouth agape, turned to our nearby mother and said, with a note of deep reproach, "Mum, you said all the monsters were dead!" And Mum, for all her facility with language and all her words of comfort, really couldn't say anything all. Instead, she helped my father work the hook out of the

---

[**] The fish is known as an Irish Lord, sometimes nicknamed a "Double Ugly": the latter name for reasons abundantly clear to anyone who has seen one.

fish's mouth. Then my father tossed the fish back into the water—ready to scare the next fisherman and convince all comers that yes, indeed: there be monsters.

Above Cook Inlet

The gray water is edged with silver lace:
the shapes of hundreds of seals
swimming in the shallows at shore's edge.

Explanation arches in deeper water:
the dark fins that travel so quickly,
waiting for the foolish or careless.

I admire the fabric of the waves,
the scenes of nature's vital drama
played out in the Inlet below.

Mephistophelean orca, dapper in black
and white, winking a huge false eye,
waits to lure the nervous everyman seals
into the colder water of his world:

his lazy swimming seems to say
he can afford to be patient.

Me versus the Silver Salmon

Silver salmon, otherwise known as coho salmon, are beautiful fish: they have bright silver scales, streamlined bodies, and tails with silver streaks that move from the base of the tail to the end, raying out in a shining sunburst. They are strong and clever creatures, known not only for their fighting ability, running out fishing lines even when they are near exhaustion, but for their wiles, such as doubling back on a run so that the line will go slack and the hook slip out, or heading for watery obstacles such as downed trees and waiting there, hoping for that moment when the line, once taut, no longer pulls them in and they can free themselves.

As a child my favorite fishing sport was silvers, and I quickly learned to never underestimate them. I still remember flying over to the Kustatan River with my dad in the PA-12, his blue and white Bush plane. The 12 was a great little plane, ideal for landing on a gravel runway or no proper runway at all, but from a passenger's perspective the 12 had one main drawback: there was a hole in the floor. The 12 seated two people in a row: the pilot in front and the passenger in back. The hole wasn't in the pilot's section but in the back, and I had to keep my feet carefully on each side of it, trying not to get too close. It was probably only a small hole, and I'm sure there was no way I could have fallen through it, but there's something unnerving about being hundreds of feet up and being able to look between your feet and see the woods and water below you.

When we arrived near the Kustatan we landed in a gravel area and walked the short way over to the river, which was wide and green. I managed to land two silvers that day, although it was hard work. My father was constantly at my side directing me about when to keep the line taut, when to let the fish play out, and how to be alert to silver tricks.

When we stayed around town, we often fished the Kenai River over at our friend Abe's house. Abe was known in some circles as "Bear Bait" because, some years before, a bear had attacked him. Abe was lucky: the bear scalped him but left him alive; his wife hiked him out to the road, flagged down a car, and got him to a hospital. Abe worked for Fish and Game and had a huge heart, as illustrated by all the work he and his wife put in to raising those triplet moose calves when a car killed the calves' mother. Abe had a classic log cabin—one of the iconic buildings of Alaska—and a great fishing spot on the banks of the Kenai River. There was a rock outcropping that created a bit of a pool to one side, and you could stand on the outcropping and either cast into the river's main flow or try the calmer waters of the pool, where salmon would sometimes rest.

We'd arrived for a full day on the Kenai, and I'd been fishing for a while with no luck when I became hungry and started dreaming of the sandwiches in my mother's picnic basket. I cast into the pool and piled rocks around the rod—my favorite, a trusty blue rod that was just the right size and weight—to keep it upright and headed a few feet up the outcropping to get a sandwich. I was sitting on the rocks contentedly eating a cheese and salami sandwich when a fish struck, and struck hard. The rod didn't twitch, it spasmed, bent nearly double, and then burst from the rocks and, as my hands grasped for it, slid into the river.

I looked after the disappearing rod in shock: not only had I lost the fish, I'd lost the rod too. I ran to tell my mother, who listened almost disbelievingly, but Abe, familiar with silver wiles, just nodded his head. He'd do what he could, he said. He began fishing in the slow-moving water near the bank, places where a fish tugging a substantial weight might hold up. He cast and cast, moving gradually along the shore until I heard a shout from him: he had the silver, still pulling my rod, on the line. Abe worked and worked that fish, gradually drawing it closer to the shore. He landed the rod but, at the last moment, the silver did what silvers do best: it slipped away, back into the silvery green river, and disappeared.

Birth River

If only I could slip into the water,
beneath that thin skin of surface,
breathe easily in the alien current—

possess gills like little red fans,
flickering slightly with each breath,
as, with one wiggle of my spine,
I glide over smooth speckled rocks—

then I could tickle the salmon,
pinch their dark mottled tails
with my small sharp teeth and lie,
companionable, in the pale green
glacial water, scenting the birth
river with my snout—

jump to complete the cycle,
laying my eggs in the shallows
then rotting, scales from my silver
skin washed up on the bank, my flesh
an eagle's meal, my bones mixing
with the driftwood, becoming at last
the stuff of a beaver's dam.

On the Slime Line

When I was fifteen years old I began working on the slime line as a bloodliner. Translation: I began work in a fish cannery that processed salmon; my job was to scoop out the bloodline, the membrane full of blood that runs along a salmon's back. It was my first job, aside from doing chores around the house or picking weeds for one of my mother's friends. To do my job I had a water-fed spoon device and, at times, a knife because sometimes the workers further up the line forgot to slit the membrane and I needed it cut so I could scoop properly. Given my age I was not supposed to work with a knife, but I did. Checking the website for Alaska labor laws I see that I couldn't have this job today: fourteen- and fifteen-year-olds are barred from cannery work (with the exception of office work) and there's a good reason for that: it's cold, long, hard work around sometimes-dangerous equipment. Tales circulated within the canneries of people losing their hands in the header, which took off the heads of the salmon, and of workers variously punctured with knives or hit by forklifts.

The actual dangers for most of us, however, were a combination of lack of sleep, too many hours on our feet, and the stink of the work, so much so that the only thing to do at the end of the season was either to save the clothes you wore for another season or, more realistically, to burn them: the smell couldn't be eradicated. My mother made me put plastic bags down in the car so that salmon guts wouldn't seep into the upholstery, and when I arrived home I had to take off my clothes in the garage, streaking into the house and straight into a warm bath of Epsom salts to soak some of the aches, along with the worst of the smell, away.

When I finished a shift I'd look at my reflection in the cannery's bathroom mirror and barely recognize myself: my apron and gloves were smeared with blood, there were spatters of who knows what on my cheeks, and long ribbons of pink guts hung in my hair despite the protection of my kerchief. Sometimes it was hard to know what part of my body hurt worse: my shoulders and arms from performing the same scooping motion over and over, my feet from standing so long in sometimes ankle-deep pools of guts and cold water, or my ears from hearing the machines grind on and from the loud squawk of the top hits radio station: a cacophony so loud that a few times I couldn't sleep after a shift due to the ringing in my ears from all that noise.

Constant exhaustion posed a problem with driving, not that I had to do that my first year in the cannery since I didn't have my license. Instead, I had to get a ride with a fellow worker or call my parents or their friends to pick me up. When I started driving myself, during cannery work in my late teens, my trips back from the cannery late at night or early in the morning, depending on my shift, caused a challenge: how not to end up in a ditch? To counteract the effects of I-must-be-unconscious-now I'd open the windows so that the cold air would pour in, turn the radio up as loud as it would go, and sing along to all the bad pop songs; however, it was always a struggle to stay awake and on the road.

For one summer my sister Jen and I got work in adjoining canneries, which was convenient for ride sharing, though we didn't do this all the time. When we did we'd usually take it in turns to drive, but one night we arrived back at the car so exhausted that neither of us wanted to drive. We settled on a compromise: I'd drive, and Jen would keep me awake, using whatever means necessary. It was the longest drive I've ever taken, even though it was only about eight miles in all, because every time I began to fall asleep Jen hit me, and she had to hit me hard because I was past even zombie-dom. We told the miles with my head nodding and then falling and Jen's hand quickly slapping as I jerked awake.

Salmon processors work on a processing line: it's a bit like Henry Ford's automobile assembly line except, of course, our job was to deconstruct the fish, moving them from overfilling plastic totes, gutting them, cleaning them, sorting them, and sending them to the freezer room to be frozen for transit, with the valuable egg sacs removed for separate sale and processing in the egg room.

As noted, my first year on the line I worked as a bloodliner, a typical job for a young, new worker. The second year my job was grab the egg sacs on the line and put them in a plastic basket, which would then go to the egg room. It was an okay job by cannery standards, though lifting the full baskets strained every part of my body and I wonder what kinds of damage I may have done to my back and knees. With an eye to even a bit more comfort, I kept trying to get a job off the line and in the egg room, with no success.

Egg room positions were considered cushier because you were away from the noise and muck of the line. The only downside of the egg room was that the Japanese foremen were very particular about the treatment of the roe and constantly critiqued the workers' sorting and packaging. The roe was packed into small wooden boxes, the thick lines of garnet- to amber-colored roe glistening like jewels. The roe was sold overseas, primarily to Japan; at that point there wasn't really a market in Alaska for it, except as bait to catch more fish. One of the foremen delighted in walking down the line eating just-cleaned roe as we watched with a mix of amazement and disgust. When my mother briefly worked at a cannery she worked in the egg room, and while she proudly notes that all of us, with the exception of my father, served time in the cannery, we girls hasten to note that of all of us she had the plum assignment.

The real smart cookie, however, was my youngest sister Rachel, who managed to gain a job on a fish site for several summers: incredibly hard work, but at least it was work outside during the beautiful, brief Alaskan summer and, as she delighted in reminding us, it was a good deal more financially lucrative than cannery work. The best job, at least money-wise, would have been to work on a fishing boat, but as girls we were barred from such positions (the reasons always being something along the line that we were too small, lacked strength, or such; however, we knew a few girls whose families owned boats and they managed just fine).

My final summer of cannery work was spent as a grader sorting salmon by quality, my favorite of all my positions. Because graders were right at the end of the line they were often separated from some of the noise and mess found higher up the line. In that cannery the fish went through a machine that cleaned them on the way to the graders, so there was less blood and guts to handle. Problems occurred, however, when the line went too fast and fish piled up on the grading table and started slipping off it, as the foremen yelled. We'd try to negotiate a more moderate pace, but if break time was coming up this didn't always work. Another problem was the machine used to clean the fish after they were beheaded and gutted: it tended to clog up. Someone, sometimes one of us graders, had to feed the fish into the cleaner one by one to make sure they were thoroughly cleaned. However, if that person went too fast the machine would eat fish and shut down. If he/she went too slowly, however, fish would back up on the line and there'd be more yelling (there was always yelling directed at someone—I just tried to make sure it wasn't always me).

At my cannery the graders sorted the fish into three grades: 1s were the best fish, frozen whole and sold to restaurants and supermarkets; 2s were good but slightly flawed and they might go to supermarkets or be canned; and 3s were more seriously flawed and were canned for human or animal consumption. You could usually tell even before you touched the fish what grade it should be, a quick eyeballing often sufficed, but touching it and checking it inside and out helped banish any doubt—although there wasn't really room for much thought given the speed at which we worked.

One day we got in a huge delivery of pink salmon (also called humpies) that were in a horrible condition. Pinks are the smallest of the five primary Alaskan salmon species, and their flesh is softer and paler than reds (sockeye) and silvers (coho). They are also the most abundant of the salmon species and the least expensive to buy. Pinks tend to go off quickly, and these pinks had obviously been caught some time ago or perhaps iced improperly. Even in the totes, covered with ice, I could see that their flesh was soft and their bodies floppy: not a good sign. There was also a distinct smell, one that we could smell even within the stink of the cannery. We told the foreman that there was no way we could grade these fish, that they were barely worthy of pet food or the compost pile, but he insisted. So, there we were trying to grade a giant, already stinking, pile of pink salmon, the fish so soft that the flesh fell away from the bone and bits of green gut material lingered inside. Every time I tried to pick one up it started to disintegrate in my hand, and I couldn't get the salmon thrown into the 3s bin fast enough, although I felt ashamed to do so: calling these pinks 3s was a decided insult to the rest of the 3s.

Despite the mind- and body-numbing nature of the work, we still managed to find things to do to amuse ourselves. One favorite game was flicking fish parts at each other: balancing a liver or a heart at the end of a knife and flicking it at an unsuspecting fellow worker as he or she flinched and then cried out in protest—ah, what joy. Another favorite pursuit was salmon tossing: taking a whole fish and tossing it at other people. If you were on the ball and managed to catch a tossed salmon, you got the gift of a whole fish, wet, cold, and slimy, in your arms. If you were inattentive, you got fish slapped. Given that we processed all kinds of salmon from the more diminutive pink and red salmon to the larger silver and dog (chum) salmon, as well as the sometimes-mammoth kings (chinooks), a fish slap was rarely a light tap. We occasionally had kings that were so large that two of us would have to carry it down the line, one girl taking the head and the other the tail.

The cannery workers consisted of locals like me, as well as people from Outside, often college students or folks making money for low-budget traveling, or people from overseas who came once for the adventure or traveled year after year to work in multiple canneries over the season, staying in cheap motels or camping. In some areas there were barracks for workers, though not in our town. I felt grateful that I wasn't living in a tent like my fellow workers: the only things that kept me going were hot baths, clean sheets on my bed, and my mother's cooking.

Talking to folks back home I hear that it's no longer common for young Alaskans to work in canneries, which seems strange to me. Like it or not, it was a huge part of growing up for coastal people. While it was boring, stinky, and pretty darn horrible, it gave me a true appreciation for just how difficult a job can be. And it serves as a great reality check: whenever I'm upset at some aspect of a recent job I think "Thank god I'm not back in the cannery," and then everything is just that little bit better.

Abundance

We were so wealthy then, although we did not know it:
moist pink-fleshed trout on our plates; a giant freezer full
of halibut and moose; the green rivers rich with salmons'
sleek bodies, their silver shingles shaking down to soft
white bellies—how many of them we pulled out and ate,
little thinking our abundance
might end.

Danger or Dinner Bell?

My parents have been close to bears in the wild a number of times; these bears were mostly black bears, and the majority of these encounters were, luckily for both my parents and the bears, not especially memorable. However, there was one instance in which this was not the case, and it occurred when they were on the second day of traveling on the thirty-nine-mile-long Resurrection Pass Trail, hiking from the town of Hope, on the south side of Turnagain Arm, to Cooper Landing, which lies close to the glorious clear green-blue waters of Kenai Lake.

It was mid-morning, and they'd been walking for some time, having camped on the trail overnight. As they walked along a ridge they sighted a brown bear below them: a sow (a female bear) with some blonde hairs mixed in with the darker hairs of her coat. The bear was grubbing: using her paws to dig for food. My parents stopped to watch; my father, rarely inclined to hyperbole, noted to me in telling the story that the bear was big, one of the biggest he'd ever seen, and beautiful.

My parents admired the bear from the height of the ridge, with a dip and a hillock between them and the sow. Dad broke the silence. "Watch this," he said, taking out his two metal Sierra Club cups, the cups we used for coffee, oatmeal, and anything else while camping. Dad planned to bang the cups together so that the bear would stand and run up the nearby hill—he couldn't resist the treat of seeing this large animal in motion. So, Dad took out the cups and clapped them together: *Bang, bang, bang!* The bear heard the noise, turned, and stood up; as she did, my parents realized how truly large she was. She looked at them, dropped to the ground, and started loping in their direction. The noise of the cups had been like a dinner bell, and she was coming for dinner.

Dad looked at the bear, thinking her strategy might be to circle around, possibly intersecting with them further down the trail. He said to Mum, "Don't run, just walk quickly." The two moved down the trail, Dad with his handgun, his 9-millimeter, ready. He knew it would be largely useless, but he touched it as they walked, trying not to put their backs to the sow. They walked rapidly in the direction they originally planned to go, and Mum finally saw the sow cross the trail and go back in the direction she had been heading when they first encountered her. After some consideration, the bear had decided that the *bang, bang, bang* of those cups was not a dinner bell after all. Even though the bear had moved away from them, Mum reported that they walked quite fast for some time, only slowing down when they finally reached a snowfield and there was no sign of her.

A guy later came down the trail and said the bear had a two-year-old cub with her whom she was carefully guarding. When the guy told Dad about the cub, he understood that the sow was actually getting them out of her territory and away from her cub and that the cup banging was a very, very bad idea. When my parents told me this story they noted that it was scary at the time, but it wasn't until afterwards, as they contemplated the sheer size and speed of the bear, that they were truly afraid, realizing that if she'd actually gone after them that they wouldn't have had a chance. As Mum said, with a small smile, "In the wild, four legs are always better than two."

The Story of Brave Bear Woman

His scalp torn off, skin broken by the bear's
yellow teeth—under the harvest moon he lies,
unmoving, and the woman beside him holds
his dark blood in the cup of her palms;
they have been married a year. Any sound
she makes will only call the bear back, so
she does not cry, barely breathes, as she rises,
lifts him, staggers forward; she knows it is miles
to the road and any chance of help.

She rests, half-falling, against a leaning spruce,
hearing his labored sounds in the cruel hush
of the cold night, wishing, perhaps, a cessation
of it all, a final relaxation, but she can't stop,
tottering onwards, each breath a wound, every muscle
knotted, she stumbles, half blind, onto the road—
a wavering shadow in the silver searchlights,
a nightmare figure on the dark black road.

Months later, they return to the forest, walking in
with the faint fall of first snow, she still limping
a bit, he with a permanently bald head; she freezes
with memory, can't believe what she did
under that full-bellied yellow moon, how
that night she was filled with a bear's might—
ferocity, blood, need—she knows she can never
explain that night to him.

Afterword

I hope that you've enjoyed this collection of stories and poems about Alaska and the animals, wild and domestic, I've known. I also hope that this collection inspires you to conserve wild places and protect these locations' animals, from the diverse creatures inhabiting the vast expanse of Alaska, stretching from the glittering snows of the Arctic to the lush forests of southeast, to the critters occupying your own backyard. With hopes for a long and healthy future for these creatures and spaces, I end with this poem.

The Snow Geese

As the last snow left the mud flats,
we saw a second snowfall cover
the brown-gray mud, float above
the steel-dull river, gilded gold
in the glow of the slight March sun.

The entire town emptied to salute
these wayfarers, traveling north
to nest on rocky shores, vast tundra.

Greedy with hunger, they lingered,
feeding on stands of swamp grass;
at a bark or a backfire, they'd rise
to wheel around us in vast gyres,
snow falling upwards, pale tempest
roaring, a dizzying, sharp cacophony

of wings, of honks: even the caribou spooked at the sound, staying sheltered in the stands of withered black spruce.

As suddenly as they came, the snowy flurry dissipated; we watched the last ones fade into the faint sunset and knew, at last, that it was almost summer time.

About the Author

K. Brenna Wardell is a writer and teacher who grew up in Alaska. She has published poetry with several small presses, and her work has been presented at Teatro Milagro in Portland, Oregon, and the Last Frontier Theatre Conference in Valdez, Alaska. She has written for publications such as the *Anchorage Daily News* and the theatre magazine *Callboard* and workshopped her poetry at the Sewanee Writers' Conference. She is currently an assistant professor at the University of North Alabama, where she teaches courses in film and literature.

www.ingramcontent.com/pod-product-compliance
Lightning Source LLC
Chambersburg PA
CBHW030451010526
44118CB00011B/882